DR. MANSOOR AL AALI
& MS. SAMIA YOUSIF

COMPUTER JOBS & CERTIFICATIONS

CHOOSE & IMPROVE YOUR **IT** CAREER

COMPUTER JOBS & CERTIFICATIONS
Choose & Improve Your IT Career

TABLE OF CONTENTS

COMPUTER JOBS & CERTIFICATIONS
Choose & Improve Your IT Career

ACKNOWLEDGMENT

We would like to thank our families for giving us the time and the support to write this book. We would like to thank our students over the years who have asked the right and inspiring questions about their careers.

COMPUTER JOBS & CERTIFICATIONS
Choose & Improve Your IT Career

CHAPTER

1 INTRODUCTION

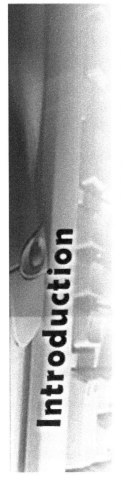

This book is an excellent choice for any person working in the field of IT or studying for an IT or IT related degree. This book was written to serve as a guide for IT professionals, IT job seekers and IT students alike. This book addresses the major challenges facing IT professionals, IT job seekers and IT students. This book will help you in planning for rewarding IT jobs.

Information Technology has by far the widest range of dynamic jobs which are forever on the increase in number, in specialty and in pay. It is by far the only field which changes in techniques, tools, technology, methodologies, theories and applications. At the same time, IT consists of a number of major components which are so independent yet fit together to create systems which today humanity cannot function without them.

IT merges hardware, operating systems, networking and programming to allow IT professionals to develop systems for almost any application. Examples of these applications are banking systems, geographical information systems, GPS systems, medical information systems, process control systems amongst many more. It can realistically be argued that IT is the field where everybody is guaranteed a job.

The field of IT consists of tens if not hundreds of different job titles which is not matched by any other field. It may even supersede the field of medicine in the number of different specializations. IT jobs are dynamic in that they develop with the technology and the products produced by major computer manufacturers, software houses as well as the different applications in industry and the public sector.

You can work as a network engineer, a computer security specialist, a software developer, a systems designer, a web developer, a graphics expert, a hardware technician, an IT manager or an IT auditor. IT itself is divided into many fields, e.g., networking, hardware, operating systems, security, systems design, project management, internet, programming, auditing, graphics, simulation, artificial intelligence, etc.

If we take the field of programming for example, we realize that this is a very dynamic field which requires programming professionals dealing with the latest development tools and programming languages. The field of programming employs programmers who intelligently develop software applications for banks, manufacturing industries, governments, supermarkets, insurance companies, airlines, and may more types of services. Since the seventies, IT has been a very dynamic field where each programming language is constantly developing and a stream of new programming language is emerging. Examples of current programming languages include C++, Java, C#, VB, ASP amongst many others. Each one of these languages has its audience and is developed by different companies. Right from the beginnings of COBOL and FORTRAN to C#.NET, the supply of good programmers has always been less than the demand and hence the great opportunities.

Another example is the field of database management systems which have become the backbone of all major commercial systems. Database management systems packages such as ORACLE and Microsoft SQL Server have been constantly developing to better versions. These packages require specialists as database administrators who are able to install and tune them and interface them with development tools and different computer networks.

The fields of systems analysis and design and project management definitely pay handsomely for professionals who master the art of system development and project management. Mastering system design methodologies and the software life cycle and converting business logic into software system logic requires mastermind professionals. Further, managing software projects is a challenging task which requires highly experienced professionals to manage software development teams, budgeting, development techniques and workflow. These professionals handle projects with budgets ranging from thousands of dollars to tens of millions of dollars and their pay package matches their expertise and capabilities.

Planning for and finding a good job in IT – Information Technology is the challenge of many people in every society and in every country. Right now tens of thousands of students are studying IT in many universities around the world. Every computer or IT student would know what constitutes the field of IT. Universities offer both undergraduate and postgraduate degrees in computer science, information systems, computer engineering, software engineering, web engineering, etc. All these degrees fall under the umbrella of IT. Computer graduates who have attained a degree in IT would know the challenges that exist for an IT student and graduate. At university they learn the basic skills such as programming, basic systems design techniques, some operating systems methods, networking and security principles, and will do a few courses here and there about computer security systems, networking systems, etc. Normally these students graduate with a great potential for a job but are not professionally equipped to deal with challenging tasks. They normally require further training and experience.

Recent IT graduates seeking IT jobs or current professionals seeking better or different jobs would normally read the newspapers, e-recruitment web sites or visit company websites. They would prepare a CV and send it highlighting their qualifications and experience and would get ready for an interview. They would compete for the best IT jobs and would have to demonstrate their skills and knowledge in their field. Employers are normally impressed by university grades only as an indication of basic knowledge and commitment. However, they would want to see further evidence that the candidate is able to work professionally. Having a professional certification would definitely prove that the candidate has what it takes to fill the job at hand. Many companies and societies offer examination to internationally recognized professional certifications. For example, ORACLE, SUN systems and Microsoft are software developers and have matching certifications for their products. Societies such as IEEE, IEE, BCS, ITPMI and many others provide professional certifications for a variety of jobs.

This book is divided into a number of chapters. Chapter 4 presents all the popular and up-to-date certifications relevant to the recent IT jobs. There are altogether twelve sections in this chapter and each section details the certifications given by a specific company, organization or society. Chapters 5 to 11 present the best and most popular IT jobs and gives important information about the job which any job seeker can identify with. These chapters also serve to help employers identify with the description of certain IT jobs. Against for each job we identified the corresponding certificate or certificates that are the most suitable for these jobs. We present a cross-reference between the job and its corresponding certification(s).

Chapters 5 to 11 present a survey and descriptions for international IT professional jobs which the job seeker can consider. These chapters cover hundreds of different IT jobs and their corresponding job titles in many IT fields such as administration, networking, security, design, databases and programming.

This book is the first of its kind to present detailed and valuable information about IT jobs and their corresponding certifications. We believe that all IT professionals, employment agencies and companies offering IT jobs would benefit from this book. The book would serve both as a reference and as a guide for all people and companies working in the IT field or using IT systems. We have included a chapter about passing an interview which would be useful for any IT job seeker.

CHAPTER

2 BE READY FOR THE INTERVIEW

2.1 Introduction

An interview is a conversation between two or more people where questions are asked to obtain information about the interviewee. The most common type of interview for assessment is a job interview between an employer and a job candidate. The goal of such an interview is to assess a potential employee to see if he/she has the technical skills, the social skills and the required level of intelligence suitable for the job in mind.

A personal interview not only gives your potential employer an opportunity to evaluate you in depth and gives you a chance to market yourself, but it also gives you the opportunity to learn much more about the employer and the company. It is important that you are able to demonstrate your abilities to the interviewer and to show them that you can do the job and that you will add value to the company and contribute to its progress and achievements.

By knowing what is expected of you and by undertaking a few simple preparations, you can make a good impression and minimize any nervousness you may feel.

With regards to information technology professionals the interviewer would normally ask questions about skills in software or hardware and about any IT experience directly related to the job in mind or in any other IT discipline of relevance to the job in mind. Questions are asked by the interviewer in a way to validate the IT skills the person has and how he or she would contribute to the company, keeping in mind the principles and goals of the organization.

Depending on the IT job you applied for or the career intended for the applicant, the questions may focus on that specific specialty or job and will include technical questions. As an applicant you have to demonstrate your technical knowledge of the field and show your competitiveness and ability to deliver the tasks that may be requested of you. Accordingly there are different fields and based on the candidate's field or career the questions will be asked to test the candidate's knowledge, performance and communication skills.

2.2 General Pattern Of Interview

The interviewing process can be scary if you don't know what to expect. To make it easier on you, keep in mind that all interviews fit a general pattern. A typical interview will last about 30 minutes, although some may be longer. A typical structure of an interview is as follows:

- *2-5 minutes:* greeting and small talk.
- *5-10 minutes:* a mutual discussion of your background and credentials as they relate to the needs of the employer. This may be done with reference to your CV.
- *2-5 minutes:* you have an opportunity to ask questions.
- *2-5 minutes:* wrap-up discusses next steps in the process.

As you can see, you have limited time to state your case. The employer may try to do most of the talking. When you answer questions or ask your own, your statements should be focused and organized, but don't be too brief. Remember this is your chance to market yourself to the employer.

Interviews can be formal and structured. Most of the questions will be designed to uncover your past behavioral patterns and will be rather rapid in pace. On the other hand, they can be informal and conversational such that the pieces of your background will be uncovered in a more random way. Let the interviewer set the tone and match your style with theirs, in accordance with your individual personality. Although there is not one way of interviewing, there are standard steps that apply to every interview process.

2.2.1 First Contact

Your initial contact may be with an employee from the personnel department who will instruct you on how to proceed with your interviewers and provide you with a preview of what to expect. Alternatively, you may meet directly with an official of the department offering the job. In both cases your greeting should include a handshake, an warm hello, and lots of eye contact. Remember you must introduce yourself.

2.2.2 The Ice Breaker

In every interview, there is a short interval before getting down to business, which is normally filled with small talk. Respond with enthusiastic and pleasant answers to remarks and questions.

2.2.3 The Interview

1. Follow the interviewer's leads, but try to get the interviewer to describe the position and the duties to you early in the interview process. This way, you may be able to apply your background, skills and accomplishments to the position.

2. Establish rapport with the interviewer. People want to hire those they feel most comfortable with.

3. Make sure that your good points come across to the interviewer in a factual, sincere manner and stress achievements. For example: systems installed, programs developed, special training received, certifications, processes developed, techniques mastered, algorithms created, plans developed, etc.

4. Respond to questions being asked as they relate to the position, or the company's needs. If asked about your background, be specific and only talk about those aspects that relate to the particular position in question.

5. If you get the impression that the interview is not going well and that you have already been rejected, do not let your discouragement show.

6. Once in a while an interviewer who is genuinely interested in you may seem to discourage you as a way of testing your reaction.

7. Avoid discussing salary at the first interview. If pressed, respond: "I would seriously consider any reasonable offer you care to make".

8. Make sure you talk about why you are interested in this position and what you can offer the company.

2.3 Preparation For The Interview

Proper preparation can make the difference between receiving and not receiving a job offer. The preparation steps are as follows:

1. **Do your Research**
   Don't interview if you haven't done your homework researching the organization before your interview. Employers are interested in candidates who ask intelligent questions and are able to make intelligent conversation based on what they know about the organization. They are equally unimpressed by candidates who know nothing about the company or the position being offered.

2. **Have a Focus**
   Think about what type of position you're seeking and what type of organization you're interested in, and consider your preferences.

3. **Bring Experience to the Table**
   Relevant work experience can give you the edge over the other candidates. Work experience will also help you focus on the type of job and work environment you want.

4. **Know Who and Where**
   Know the exact place and time of the interview, the interviewer's full name, the correct pronunciation and his or her title. Find out how many people are involved in the interviewing process and who the final decision maker is.

5. **Ask Questions**
   Be prepared to ask questions during the interview. Your questions allow the hiring manager to evaluate your professional and personal needs. Insightful questions help both of you determine if your relationship will be mutually rewarding. Delay till the end the questions that relate to salary, benefits, vacations, and retirement.

6. **Keep your Timing**

   Allow sufficient time for the interview. Plan to arrive early for your actual appointment. There is no excuse for arriving late for an interview or being in a hurry to leave.

7. **Dress Appropriately**

   Dress appropriately and professionally for the interview, remember that there is only one chance to make a good first impression.

8. **Keep a Positive Frame of Mind**

   Relax and set other concerns aside and focus on what you are going to accomplish at the interview.

2.4 What Interviewers Will Be Ready For?

2.4.1 Comb Through The Resumes

Resumes/CVs can be written in different formats and many interviewers give a resume only a quick review. After all, there's no easy way to evaluate the information prior to the interview. Even if the qualifications and accomplishments could be verified, what really matters is how the candidate responds to verbal questioning or in some cases a written technical test.

However, a great deal of useful information can be deduced from a close review of a resume. The general organization, format and size of the document may reveal how applicant characteristics such as orderliness, accuracy and succinctness.

In this day and age you might think that spelling and grammar errors are things of the past but still many resumes in recent years are submitted with glaring typo errors still in them. These easy to avoid errors are worth the effort because a well written and formatted resume will make an impression. Normally the content of the resume is what would be focused on most. Make sure that information such as names, titles of degrees, titles of professional certifications, dates of graduation and work experience periods are correct and in the right order.

2.4.2 Prepare For A Team

Many interviews involve two people questioning an applicant. Interviewers normally collaborate ahead of time as to how they would question the applicant, this process seems to progress more effectively and generate better results.

2.4.3 Be Ready For Short And Open-Ended Questions Extensively

During an interview you may have to face both closed and open ended questions. Experienced interviewers tend not ask open ended question or questions which have a yes or no answers. Even seasoned interviewers fall into asking closed-end questions that can be answered in one word. Interviewers will have the technique to create questions which tests your knowledge or experience without resorting to closed or open questions. For example, instead of "Have you ever installed Windows?" you might be asked: "What versions of Windows have you recently installed and what would you do differently now?" You may be asked to 'describe how' to perform a certain task rather than 'what' to perform. Another example question is "What programming language you would use for a new web applica-

tion?" or "What system development methodology have you used in your last system development and how suitable did you find it and what alternatives are there?" The interview will of course include non-technical questions to find out about your behavioral patterns and how they would expect you to fit in with others in the company. Questions such as "Why do you want to work for us?", or "What would you do if you find out that you have made a big mistake?", or "When would you fire a lazy subordinate?" are a sample of personality mining questions.

2.4.4 Use A Familiar Name To Stop Ramblers

Fast, direct, organized and careful answers to questions are much better than rambling. If you are not sure about the answer to a question, then simply explain that you do not know or are unclear about the answer. One of the most challenging dilemmas which may face an interviewer is an applicant who rambles on and on. The applicant may be naturally long-winded, or may be nervous about the interview process. Experienced interviewers quickly notice candidates who ramble on when confronted with a question they can't quite respond to but are unwilling, or unable, to simply say "I don't know".

People tend to have internal antennae finely tuned to the sound of their name. The most effective way a seasoned interviewer will stop a rambler cold is by firmly announcing his/her first name. In most cases the rambler will pause. When you are stopped by calling your first name or some other way, that momentary interruption, is all you need to clarify your response, to summarize your rambling up to that point, or to shift the interview into a different direction.

2.4.5 Follow-up On References

References are people that you have either worked with, or your most recent manager or a lecturer at your college. Choose your references carefully. They should be people that you trust, who know you well, and can give a respectful reference which will work in your favor and their opinions will be respected by the interviewers. References can give candid opinions about your characteristics including personality traits, work habits, interpersonal and social skills, attendance and even health situation. Most applicants offer references upon request. Some interviewers feel references will only give biased, positive accounts about the applicant but that frequently is not the case.

2.5 What Interviewers Do In An Interview?

- Make notes of the questions they intend to ask and put comments on your response to these questions for referencing later.
- Decide the essential things they need to learn and prepare questions to probe them.
- Plan the environment - privacy, no interruptions, ensure the interviewee is looked after while the candidate is waiting.
- Arrange the seating in an informal relaxed way. Normally interviewers don't sit behind a desk directly facing the interviewee – they sit around a coffee table or meeting room table.
- They clear their desk, apart from what they need for the interview, so it shows they have prepared and are organized, which shows they respect the situation and the interviewee.

- Put the interviewee at ease –they know that it is stressful for you.
- Begin by explaining clearly and concisely the general details of the organization and the role.
- May ask open-ended questions - how, why, tell me, what, (and to a lesser extent where, when, which) to get you talking.
- Make sure that you do 90% of the talking.
- They will fire calm, relaxed, gentle and clever questions because they are far more revealing. High pressure causes people to clam up and rarely exposes hidden issues.
- Probe the resume/application form to clarify any unclear points.
- Give interviewees opportunities to ask their own questions.
- Questions asked by interviewees are usually very revealing. They also help good candidates to demonstrate their worth, especially if the interviewer has not asked great questions or there is a feeling that a person has for any reason not had the chance to show their real capability and potential.

2.6 Evaluations Made By Interviewers

The employer will be observing and evaluating you during the interview. Some evaluations made by the employer during the interview include:

- How mentally alert and responsive is the job candidate?
- Is the applicant able to draw proper inferences and conclusions during the course of the interview?
- Does the applicant demonstrate a degree of intellectual depth when communicating, or is his/her thinking shallow and lacking depth?
- Has the candidate used good judgment and common sense regarding life planning up to this point?
- What is the applicant's capacity for problem-solving activities?
- How well does the candidate respond to stress and pressure?

2.7 Sample Questions By Interviewers

2.7.1 General Questions

1. Why do you want to work here?
2. What kind of experience do you have for this job?
3. What did you like/dislike about your last job?
4. Why are you leaving your present position?
5. How long would you stay with the company?
6. Have you done the best work you are capable of doing?
7. How long would it take you to make a contribution to our company?
8. What would you like to be doing five years from now?
9. What are your biggest accomplishments?
10. Can you work under pressure?
11. How much money do you want?
12. What are you looking for in your next job?
13. Describe a difficult problem you've had to deal with?

2.7.2 Preparing For The Interview

1. Proper preparation can make the difference between receiving and not receiving a job offer.
2. Do some research about the company (size, products, annual sales revenue, principal lines of business and locations, etc). This will not only make you feel more comfortable during the interview, but it will also prepare you to show genuine interest in the company.
3. Know the exact place and time of the interview, the interviewer's full name, the correct pronunciation and his or her title. Find out how many people are involved in the interviewing process and who the final decision maker is.
4. Be prepared to ask questions during the interview. Your questions allow the hiring manager to evaluate your professional and personal needs. Insightful questions help both of you determine if your relationship will be mutually rewarding. Avoid questions that relate to salary, benefits, vacations, and retirement.
5. Allow sufficient time for the interview. Plan to arrive exactly ten minutes before your actual appointment. There is no excuse for tardiness at an interview.
6. Dress appropriately. Plan how you will dress for the interview, remember that there is only one chance to make a good first impression. Men should wear a dark suit, white shirt, a solid or striped tie, and black shoes. Women should wear a knee length skirted suit or tailored dress with matching jacket, neutral colored sheer hose, dark pumps, and a minimum of make-up and jewelry.
7. Keep a positive frame of mind. Set other concerns aside and focus on what you are going to accomplish at the interview.

2.8 Mistakes Made By The Interviewees

2.8.1 Dressing Unprofessionally

- The first impression is the last impression. The first thing the interviewer looks at is your way of dressing and if your dressing style is shabby then you're marked down that very instant and the chances of getting the job offer is less.
- It is always good to dress professionally when meeting representatives of the company.
- It is not necessary to look like celebrities as they often portray on T.V or on the front cover of the magazines but it is always better to have a simple and neat appearance.
- Casual dressing like jeans, bandana on the forehead, wearing caps, faded T-shirts are mistakes that sometimes candidates tend to make.
- Avoid wearing too much of ornaments or jewelry or use too much of perfume.
- Dressing style for Men would be to wear a dark suit, white shirt, a solid or striped tie, and black shoes. Women should wear a knee length skirted suit or tailored dress with matching jacket.

2.8.2 Arriving Unprepared

- An interview is an opportunity to sell yourself and your skills to a manager who is going to hire you, so be prepared for every meeting. If you don't know what products or services a company sells or what position you're interviewing for, you won't seem interested.

- It helps to know more about the company and to have done background research. This shows you're truly interested in the job.
- Before arriving for the interview, make sure you know what your goals for your career are and the requirements needed to get the available or vacant job so that you can discuss these topics with the interviewer.
- It is always a good practice to carry an extra copy of your resume to give to the interviewer and it should have the names, addresses and phone numbers of references, in case you have to complete a job application form.

2.8.3 Discussing Compensation Too Soon

- During the first interview it is not good to ask the employer about your salary package. This may give the impression that you are more concerned about your needs and not the company and as a result you may not be called for a second interview.
- Aim to tell the employer what you can do for them and not what the company can do for you.
- Employers want to know what you can contribute to the company. If you have the right skills and qualifications, you'll receive an offer and then you may negotiate a competitive package. To negotiate well, you have to research the market and know your real worth.

2.8.4 Acting Desperate

- Acting desperate is to show willingness to accept any job and any salary. It is always better to relax, stay calm, and have self control and most importantly show confidence when meeting employers.
- Do not let the fact that you are exhausted after trying for many jobs or you are burdened financially to accept any offer.
- Avoid saying that "I am over qualified" because the company has read your CV and knows your qualification.
- Always know what you want and be sure the positions you apply for meet these requirements.
- The company wants to get you excited about the position. They don't want someone who's desperate and willing to do anything.

2.8.5 Appearing Too Nervous

- Maintain a good rapport with the interviewer. Employers would like to hire those people who they feel they will be comfortable working with.
- Take down notes during the interview regarding the role of the job and the responsibilities so that you will not forget as to what was discussed the previous day at the interview.
- Always maintain a steady body posture, good eye contact. Nervous habits like biting your nails, trembling in your seat, playing with your hair or tapping your foot should be avoided.

- The interviewer knows that all candidates get nervous but it's always recommended not to make it too obvious. Best practice is to hold a pen in the hand which will divert your attention of nervousness towards the pen.
- One should always view the interview in a different perspective. They should be happy to boast about their experience and achievements. By preparing thoroughly, you'll avoid making common interview mistakes.

2.8.6 Other Negative Questions

Generally speaking the questions mentioned below suggest to the interviewer that the candidate is mostly interested in what the organization can give the employee, rather than the other way around. Interviewers want to meet and recruit interviewees who see things in terms of what the employee can do for the organization.

1. How many weeks holiday do I get?
2. When would I get a pay-rise?
3. What are the lunch times?
4. What sort of car do I get?
5. What other benefits are there?
6. What are the pension arrangements?
7. Do you have a grievance procedure?
8. What expenses can I claim for?
9. How soon before I could get promoted?
10. When is going-home time?
11. And others like these.

2.9 Questions To Ask At The Interview

1. Always prepare a list of questions to ask the interviewer. The questions that job candidates ask at the interview provide valuable insights as to their attitude, maturity, capability and strategic understanding of their role and the organization.
2. As the interviewee, take full advantage of opportunities to ask good questions. Asking good well-prepared and researched questions is your chance to demonstrate that you are better than the other candidates.
3. It is always better to ask questions at the interview rather than waiting for the interviewer to ask you the questions that you are expecting to answer and then later on regretting that you did not have the chance to show the employer your worth.
4. Always make sure you ask questions that will impress the interviewer. Avoid asking regular or routine details like the terms and conditions which will be provided in due time anyway.
5. Try to prepare and ask questions that make the interviewers think to themselves; that's a good question this candidate has really thought about the role, and understands the sort of issues we need them to handle or the sort of responsibilities or initiatives we want them to take.
6. Think before the interview about what the successful candidate will be like - ask yourself beforehand, what great questions would the successful candidate ask? And then be that person.

7. When you research the job look into the sort of challenges the organization is facing, and think how this affects the vacant role. What does the employer need from the successful applicant?

8. One can think of how he can contribute towards the roles of the organization and also show the positive nature that he has which he feels might make a difference to that particular job he or she is applying for.

2.10 Examples Of Good Questions To Ask Interviewers

These types of questions are certainly appropriate for interviewees to ask an interviewer. They are as follows:

1. What would some of my responsibilities be?
2. How would my performance be evaluated?
3. Is there room for promotion?
4. Would there be any travel involved with this position
5. Where do you see this company in two years?
6. Describe your management style?
7. How do you see me fitting into this company?

2.11 Closing The Interview

1. The closing phase is the most important part of the interview for making a lasting impression that can place you above other competitors for the same position.
2. Let the interviewer know that you are excited about the position.
3. Find out what the next step is.
4. Make a statement that indicates that you can do the job, and that you would like to receive an offer. Always ask about the offer.
5. Finally, as you are preparing to leave, express your interest to work with the employer.
6. You should expect to be dismissed or taken to another interviewer. All interviews should be handled in the same fashion. You must convince all parties in the interview process that you are the right person for the job.
7. The candidate that shows the most enthusiasm for the job, the opportunity and the company, in addition to other relevant capabilities, is usually the one that gets the offer.

2.12 Candidates Should Have

As an IT professional you should have:

1. Academic and professional qualifications.
2. Positive attitude.
3. Interest in the position and company.
4. Stable work history, if available.
5. Clear sense of purpose.
6. Communication skills.

7. High performance standards.

2.12.1 Remember Employers Need From You

1. Qualifications – A track record of success in previous roles; academic qualifications are only one part of the equation.
2. Positive Attitude – Can do, upbeat and optimistic.
3. Interest in the Company and Position – Do some research on the company before you go to the interview; show a genuine interest.
4. Stable Work History – If you have many job changes on your CV, make sure that you can justify them.
5. Clear Sense of Purpose – Do you really know: what you have achieved/what your career objectives are?
6. Communication Skills – Articulate, persuasive and convincing.
7. High Performance Standards – How principled are you? Do your principles match with those of the company you are applying to? Do you set high standards?

2.13 Methodology

First Question: "Why do you want to work here?"
To answer this question, you must have researched the company. You should reply with the company's attributes as you see them. Cap your answer with reference to your belief that this can provide you with a stable and happy work environment.

Second Question: "How long would you stay with the company?"
The interviewer might be thinking of offering you a job, but, employers are aware that the marketplace is such that new recruits often do not stay with the company more than two years. Your reply might be: "I would really like to settle down with this company, as long as I am growing professionally, there is no reason for me to make a move".

Third Question: "What did you like/dislike about your last job?"
Most interviews start with a preamble by the interviewer about his company. Pay attention: this information will help you answer the question. In fact, any statement the interviewer makes about the job or corporation can be used to your advantage. Use this to highlight all the positives of your last job. Criticizing a prior employer is a warning flag that you could be a problem employee. Keep your answers short and positive.

2.14 Tricky Questions

2.14.1 Planner or Spontaneous
When you go on holiday, what do you prefer to do?
- Plan every detail in advance.
- Plan a rough itinerary in advance, leaving some time free.
- Look at a few options in advance, but only really decide when you're there.
- You rarely plan, just book at the last minute and go with the flow.

What statement best describes how you do your regular grocery shop?
- You make a detailed list of everything you need to buy.

- You make a rough list to jog your memory.
- You don't make a list, as you think it's a waste of time.
- You don't do regular shop, you just go when you need to.

You've been to a furniture store and have come back with some flat-pack furniture, like a wardrobe or a desk that you have to assemble. What are you most inclined to do?

- Before you start, you check that all the components are there and that you have the tools you will need.
- You read through the instructions carefully first and then follow them step by step.
- You scan the instructions, although you don't always follow them exactly.
- You leap in, only referring to the instructions if you get stuck.

Which description fits you best?

- You are a perfectionist and can't leave anything unfinished.
- You need time, over-prepare and hate pressure.
- You're scatty, forgetful and disorganized.
- You put things off till the last minute and are often late.

What happens when your local supermarket moves the food to different aisles?

- You would notice and it would really bother you.
- You would notice, but you simply change the order in which you shop.
- You would notice, but it wouldn't bother you as you have no set routine.
- You probably wouldn't notice.

2.14.2 Personality

Of the following options which one describes you best?

- Realistic.
- Efficient.
- Imaginative.
- Visionary.

How do you usually give directions to your house? Do you...

- Provide a step-by-step list of directions for the entire journey?
- Draw a really detailed map that shows things like street names and roundabouts?
- Just give general directions?
- Sketch a rough map, as too many details can be confusing?

Which set of words best describes you?

- Practical, thorough and stable.
- Realistic, enthusiastic and spontaneous.
- Inventive, imaginative and original.
- Creative, dynamic and adventurous.

Which of these best describes how you do your supermarket shopping?

- You usually go up and down the aisles in exactly the same order.
- You read and compare labels and prices.
- You're attracted to new things or special offers that catch your eye.
- You vary the way you go round the supermarket depending on what you feel like buying.

2.14.3 Heads Or Hearts

Which set of words best describe you?
- Analytical, logical and objective.
- Decisive, driven and energetic.
- Caring, helpful and supportive.
- Complex, thoughtful and sensitive.

What would you do if you had to decide between two homes to move into?
- List your ideal features and compare which place has the most.
- Compare the good and bad features of both.
- Go with your gut feeling about which is best.
- Think about how each place affects the other people in your life.

If your friend wanted to marry someone you really disliked and asked you what you thought about their marriage, what would you do?
- Be up front and honest about what you think.
- Try to be tactful - but still be truthful about what you think.
- Try not to hurt their feelings, changing the subject if necessary.
- Avoid hurting their feelings, telling a "white lie" if necessary.

If you are with a group of friends and an argument breaks out, what do you tend to do?
- Face the dispute head on.
- Try to find an answer to the problem.
- Try to meet everyone's needs.
- Anything to avoid hurting people's feelings.

When you have to make a difficult decision, what is most important to you?
- Arriving logically at the best choice.
- Being as fair as possible.
- Doing the right thing according to your own beliefs and values.
- Getting the approval and agreement of others.

2.14.4 Extrovert Or Introvert

When you are out with a group of your friends, how much of the talking do you usually do?
- Hardly any at all.
- A little less than most.
- Quite a lot.
- Almost all.

When it comes to expressing yourself do you...
- Hold back more, listening to others before speaking?
- Think before you speak?
- Think out loud?
- Use your hands and facial expressions a lot?

What are you like when you have to meet a group of new people?
- You stick with the people you've met before.
- You spend your time thinking about how to keep the conversation going.

- You aim to mingle with as many new people as possible.
- You just go out and have fun.

Which set of words best describes you?
- Cautious, thoughtful and loyal.
- Inquisitive, independent and contained.
- Lively, enthusiastic and energetic.
- Expressive, talkative and friendly.

If you are in the middle of something important and the phone rings how do you usually react? Do you...
- Ignore the phone, or let the machine pick up?
- Take the call, but deal with it as quickly as possible?
- Answer it as you welcome the chance to talk to someone, but keep it brief?
- Answer the phone enthusiastically and be up for a long conversation?

2.15 More IT Related Questions

1. Why did you decide to get a computer science degree?
2. Why did you choose computer science over computer engineering?
3. What do you most enjoy about being a developer?
4. What is most challenging about web development?
5. What type of personality is a good fit for a computer programmer?
6. What are your career goals?
7. What advice do you have for people interested in going into computer programming and web development?
8. How did you get into web design?
9. What do you most enjoy about designing a site?
10. How do you work with clients?
11. What's the most challenging part of your job?
12. What does a person coming into this field need to know?

CHAPTER

3 WHY & HOW TO GET IT CERTIFICATION

3.1 Introduction

It is very important for you as a computer professional to get a computer/IT certification from a reputable organization and in the right discipline. Certification will make you more visible to employers and colleagues, will create better opportunities for you, and will help you to get more offers for more and better jobs. Although you know your own capability and in some cases the employer will recognize that you have the required skills necessary to do the job, they will have better confidence in you if you are certified and will feel more confident to offer you the job or promotion. In some cases it works just like a driving license, you do not ask someone to demonstrate that they can drive; you just ask them to produce their driving license.

A college degree is definitely an asset and indicates achievement, dedication, knowledge of the field as well as many other academic and non-academic skills. However, a college degree is not always enough to impress an employer that the candidate has the potential to fill the job at hand.

A college degree normally indicates that the candidate will have the required intelligence and basic knowledge to be employed and the job may be offered to him/her in the absence of someone else with the right degree, certification and may be experience. When a college degree is coupled with one or two years of experience, it gives that extra bit of assurance to the employer that the candidate is a safe bet to employ. However, an international certification is a guaranteed way to impress the employer that you have what it takes to occupy a professional job, that you are certified by an international organization and that you have the capability to deliver, and most importantly that you are licensed to do the job.

International computer/IT certification can help you in a number of ways:

- Gives the public who deal with you, in this case the computer systems users, the confidence that they are dealing with a certified professional.
- Provides a proof to other professionals in the field that you have the skills to match the job you occupy or will occupy.
- Helps you to compete with other professionals to get the best job because it makes you stand out from the crowd.
- Gives the employer and the public as well as yourself the confidence that you are staying up-to-date with the latest development in IT technology, techniques, products, etc.
- Helps you when you want to switch between jobs to demonstrate that you have not been using old technology or old techniques during your previous job.
- Proves that you are the kind of person who likes to be the best at what you do.
- Helps you to acquire and increase your skills and qualifications necessary for addressing career development.
- Certification can become a way of life. Certification helps you to stay abreast of developments, be competent, use the correct techniques, prove that you have the knowledge and intelligence and the speed to deliver tasks correctly, efficiently and on time and to the right budget.

If you are interested in a career in IT, or you are already in IT then definitely a college degree and an international certification is the right combination and the correct way forward for you. You need to plan your career and choose the right certification. To start with visit the web sites of the most famous certification sponsors and software producers such as Oracle, Cisco, Sun, CompTIA, Microsoft, Linux, Novell, and other vendors and testing centers.

It is easy to get frustrated because of not knowing how to move forward. An informed decision from a forum, a consultant, a colleague or from any other professional sources should definitely be a welcome guide. Looking at e-recruitment websites for "hot jobs", reading professional computer magazines and generally observing the job market is a must before you make the decision to move forward and get certified. You have to know your capabilities, your selected growth path and the career opportunities available.

3.2 Training And Certification

Training gives you the chance to advance your career. What training you need to get certified in and where to get it from is a major question about IT certification. You must research what jobs are available, what certifications they need, where to get trained, and where to get certified from. A carefully studied decision is absolutely important. It is of no use if you spend your money, your time, your effort in getting certified in a branch of IT or in a tool or in a package that is on the way out of the market. It is equally important to get certified in a "hot job" which guarantees you a better financial offer. Train with the vendor or institute which has a better turnout of certified professionals. A training organization must have the qualified and experienced trainers, the right set up and the skills necessary to give you a smooth ride to get your certification. The issue of cost is too obvious to discuss.

Example of selected IT jobs which require certifications:

Networking

Networking provides big and numerous opportunities for IT professionals. It is a vast and diverse field and offers enough jobs for those interested. A job in networking could be one of many types available. Examples of networking tasks could be to install networks or deal with networking security issues. There are many networking products from different vendors, each of which requires trained and certified professionals. The Networking industry is huge with many companies and a big range of technologies. Of the entire IT career fields currently available, few can offer the diversity that computer networking provides.

Programming

Being a programmer means the ability to learn a modern programming language, use this language to develop software products which require logic development. You have to know what does it take to become a software developer. It involves developing logic, creating algorithms, debugging syntax and logical bugs in the program, and integrating products and tools. Programming/Software Engineering plays a vital role in the IT industry and offers a variety of jobs. It is important to note that new and more modern programming tools and languages appear every year. If you have a clear mind, know how to solve logical problems and you are an algorithmic thinker, then definitely this is a job for you.

DBA

A Database Administrator job is a senior job in the IT industry. Normally a DBA is responsible for installing database products such as ORACLE and SQL Server, tune these products, develop backup and recovery procedures, integrate database systems with other computer software and operating systems, and have knowledge of database security. This is normally a senior position. However, there aren't as many DBA jobs as networking and programming jobs.

Example of selected IT certification vendors:

CCNA

CCNA Cisco Certified Network Associate is a certification by Cisco which mostly deals with Cisco networking and network security products. If you are interested in a career in networking then definitely CCNA and Cisco are a good choice. Prospective IT certification candidates normally start with Cisco's foundation program.

A+

A+ is an independent certification organization which certifies the competency of service professionals in the computer industry. A+ is one of the most popular and widely recognized certifications especially for technical support and PC maintenance.

Project+

IT projects can cost millions, require careful management of resources and products and need to be delivered within time scales. IT project management is a field for senior IT professionals and consultants which have high financial rewards. Project+ is one of many types of IT project management certifications to consider if you have been a developer and have worked as a systems analyst and you are now ready to take on this challenging task.

3.3 General Advice About Jobs & Certifications

1. Before you start a career in IT or change from one IT specialty to another, you should have a reasonable idea of the requirements of the area you're interested in.
2. Qualification, certification and experience are the three major factors for getting a good job in IT, but your personality, your enthusiasm, your commitment and your potential growth are other major factors to consider.
3. As the saying goes "failing to plan is planning to fail". Career planning is important. You could easily sit comfortably in one field or job and not realize that this field is fading away and giving way to new technologies, tools, techniques, methodologies, etc.
4. Choosing a certification is not based on guising, it is based on real information realized by searching for the correct information from a good source. It is good advice to review and analyze trends that will affect your career plans.

3.4 Most Frequently Asked Questions

Newly graduated or about to graduate IT professionals as well as IT professionals already employed as well as IT managers all have questions to ask about IT jobs and IT certifications. We have tried to group the most important questions which IT professionals or potential professionals may want to ask.

1. Why should I get an IT certification?

IT Certification provides an independent verification of a certain level of expertise (skills and knowledge) in a particular area of Information Technology. The programs are meant to identify the necessary skills for an individual to perform their job competently. IT certifications specialize in a specific area of IT such as programming in a given language such as C#. Technical areas include Database Administration, Programming, Engineering, Networking and Internetworking. It provides professionals with recognized and valued qualifications or licenses.

2. Where do I get my certification?

IT certifications can be obtained from different sources. You can obtain a certification from the product developer, eg, ORACLE or Microsoft. You can also obtain your certification from an independent body, eg, CompTIA. Certification providers could provide you with the certification only or the training and certification.

3. What is the procedure for getting certified?
1. Identify your career or employment plans.
2. If you are already employed, evaluate your current employment situation.
3. Realize the costs involved in terms of time, money and effort.
4. Study the different certification options available.
5. Study and realize the real benefits and implications of the certification.
6. Carefully choose the certification which will give you the maximum benefits.
7. Search for the best training providers to get your certification.

8. Do not just remember the material of the training, study the material and assess yourself by doing practical exercises. Hands-on experience will be a major advantage.

9. Once you feel that you are ready, register and pay for the exam at one of the available exam centers.

4. What are the resources available to help me to get certified?

- Internet forums and discussion groups.
- World Wide Web certification sites.
- Online training.
- Training at training centers.
- Materials provided by the certification sponsor.
- Study guides and textbooks.
- Self-assessment tests.
- Friends already certified in the same field.

5. What are the popular certifications?

- Oracle Corporation, eg, Oracle Database Administrator Certified Professional (OCP).
- Cisco Systems, eg, Cisco Certified Network Associate (CCNA).
- Microsoft Corporation, eg, Microsoft Certified System Engineer (MCSE).
- Computing Technology Industry Association (CompTIA), eg, A+.
- Sun Microsystems, eg, Sun Certified Java Programmer.

6. Are there examples of popular certifications?

- Microsoft MCSD
- Microsoft MCDBA
- Microsoft MCP
- Microsoft MCSE
- Microsoft MCSA
- Microsoft MCS
- Microsoft MCP
- Cisco CCNA
- Cisco CCNP
- Cisco CCIE
- Cisco CCDA
- ISC2 CISSP
- ISC2 SSCP
- CompTIA Network+
- CompTIA A+
- PMP

7. Which is better: a degree or a certification?

A degree is expected to develop you intellectually and mentally and to impart the required knowledge for a particular field. On the other hand, certification is intended to make someone an expert in a particular product or field, so as to make you skillful in that particular product or field. We will argue that it is best to get both simultaneously or get certified after graduation from your degree.

8. Can I study for the certification on my own and take the exam?

Anybody can select the certification, choose the right training material, study the material, do practice tests, and then sit for the test. However, this could be a difficult task due to your other commitments and some topics may prove to be difficult to understand and require an instructor for guidance.

9. What if I do not get my certification and just depend on my work experience?

Certification can be viewed as the shortest and easiest way of getting recognized by the IT employers. It can stimulate your skills and intelligence. It will point you in the right direction.

10. What are the types of exam formats in use?

Professional IT certifications have similar formats. They are normally conducted over the Internet in a recognized testing centre. Some tests can take the form of multiple choice questions or giving a one word solution to a problem, or by filling in the blanks. Occasionally, some tests can take the form of an adaptive format where the candidate will be started with questions of average difficulty and the next question will be made easier or more difficult depending on the answers of the student. The idea is to decide the exact capability and the level of the candidate.

11. Do I need hands-on experience before I take a certification exam?

Most certifications are for specific products, technologies, software systems, methodologies, tools, etc. The theoretical part is limited, but the way to handle the tool or product and apply it is the main requirement. Therefore, hands-on experience is a must for most certifications.

12. Where can an IT certified professional work?

An IT certified professional can work in IT software houses, banks, manufacturing companies, service companies, cybercafés, business centers, internet service providers, educational institutions, oil and gas companies, government establishments, ministries, computer vendors, etc. Depending on your qualifications, specialization and certifications, you can work as a programmer, a software engineer, a networking engineer, an information security specialist, a hardware technician, a database administrator, instructor/trainer, etc. You can also set up on your own.

13. What are the common certification mistakes to avoid?

- Underestimating the cost of time, effort and money.
- Not carefully researching for the right certification for you.
- Not taking the practical element of the exam seriously.
- Choosing a certification just because it is easy and not because it is useful for you.
- Not taking the most up-to-date certification.
- Not selecting the most competitive training centre.

14. Why are certification exams updated? And what is re-certification?

Because knowledge within the IT industry is dynamic and rapidly changing, certifications will be updated to address new and emerging technologies. Program updates are based on the need to improve the certification quality using industry feedback and developments in the IT industry.

Recertification is related to program updates and is a requirement for certification sponsors who time-limit their certifications. Again the essence is to demonstrate an ongoing commitment to knowledge acquisition and the maintenance of continuing competence. Some vendors believe that it is essential to certify that the certification holder is keeping up with current trends in the industry.

CHAPTER

4 IT CERTIFICATIONS

4.1 Cisco Certifications

Cisco enables people to make powerful connections-whether in business, education, philanthropy, or creativity. Cisco hardware, software, and service offerings are used to create the Internet solutions that make networks possible-providing easy access to information anywhere, at any time.

Cisco was founded in 1984 by a small group of computer scientists from Stanford University. Since the company's inception, Cisco engineers have been leaders in the development of Internet Protocol (IP)-based networking technologies. Today, with more than 63,000 employees worldwide, this tradition of innovation continues with industry-leading products and solutions in the company's core development areas of routing and switching, as well as in advanced technologies.

http://www.cisco.com

C001 Cisco Certified Design Associate (CCDA)

Description
Students analyze a customer's existing internet-work and determining present and future customer needs. Based on this analysis, each student will design network solutions that include the network topology, LAN and WAN hardware and media, network-layer addressing, routing protocols, software feature provisioning, and a network management strategy. When the design is complete, students will learn how to create and present an internet-work design document to the customer, and then prove to the customer that the design works based on a prototype or pilot.

You must pass Designing Cisco Networks (DCN) exam. You must also sign the Cisco Career Certifications Agreement. You must recertify every three years by taking the same exam. Alternatively, if a recertification candidate passes any new exam at the professional or Cisco Qualified Specialist level; the candidate will also be considered recertified at the CCDA level. Passing any CCIE written exam will recertify Cisco Qualified specialist, associate and professional level certifications.

Skill Level: Basic

C002 Cisco Certified Design Professional (CCDP)

Description
For individuals who design complex routed LAN, routed WAN and switched LAN networks of 100 to more than 500 nodes that utilize Cisco routers and switches. To earn the CCDP you must first earn the CCDA and CCNA certifications. You must then pass three additional exams: Building Scalable Cisco Internet works (BICSI); Building Cisco Multilayer Switched Networks (BCMSN); and Designing Cisco Network Architectures (ARCH). You must also sign the Cisco Career Certifications Agreement. You can elect to take the composite exam in place of the BSCI and BCMSN exams, shortening the path to certification by one exam. You must recertify every three years by passing the then applicable CCDP recertification exam. Passing any CCIE written exam will recertify Cisco Qualified specialist, associate and professional level certifications.

Skill Level: Intermediate

C003 Cisco Certified Internet-work Expert (CCIE)

Description
For computer professionals who wish to demonstrate internetworking expertise. This top-of-the-line certification is for individuals who work specifically with Cisco products. It is currently one of the premiere IT certifications. You must first pass a written exam computer based test administered. Then you must also pass a hands-on practical lab at a Cisco testing facility. You must attempt the lab exam within 18 months of passing the written exam. There are five CCIE tracks to choose from: Routing and Switching; Security; Service Provider; Storage Networking, and Voice. Every two years after becoming certified, CCIE must recertify by passing any CCIE qualification exam.

Skill Level: Advanced

C004 Cisco Certified Internetwork Professional (CCIP)

Description

For individuals who work in an end-to-end Cisco environment, covers IP routing, IP multicast, cable, DSL, content networking or IP telephony. You must first hold Cisco CCNA certification. Then you must pass four exams: Building Scalable Cisco Networks (BSCI); Implementing Cisco Quality of Service (QoS); Implementing Cisco MPLS (MPLS) and Configuring BGP on Cisco Routers (BGP). You must recertify every three years. CCIP recertification can also be accomplished by passing the BGP+MPLS exam; or by passing both the BGP and MPLS exams.

Skill Level: Intermediate

C005 Cisco Certified Network Associate (CCNA)

Description

For individuals who install, configure, and operate LAN, WAN and dial access services for small networks (100 nodes or fewer), including but not limited to use of these protocols: IP, IGRP, IPX, Serial, AppleTalk, Frame Relay, IP RIP, VLANs, RIP, Ethernet, Access Lists, using Cisco routers and switches. There are two paths to certification - a one exam path and a two exam path. The paths cover the same material. For the one exam path you must pass the current CCNA exam. The two exam path breaks the topics covered into two exams, one being more introductory.

The two exams are: INTRO (Introduction to Cisco Networking Technologies) and ICND (Interconnecting Cisco Network Devices). If using the two exams path both exams must be taken within three years of each other. You must also agree to the Cisco Career Certifications and Confidentiality Agreement. You must recertify every three years by passing the CCNA or ICND exam. Alternatively, if a recertification candidate passes any new exam at the professional or Cisco Qualified Specialist level; the candidate will also be considered recertified at the CCNA level.

Skill Level: Basic

C006 Cisco Certified Network Professional (CCNP)

Description

This designation is for individuals who install, configure, operate, and troubleshoot LAN, WAN, and Dial Access Services that utilize Cisco routers and switches, for organizations with networks from 100 to more than 500 nodes. This is the next step after CCNA certification. You must hold CCNA. You must also pass four more exams: Building Scalable Cisco Internetwork (BSCI); Building Cisco Multilayer Switched Networks (BCMSN); Building Cisco Remote Access Networks (BCRAN); and Cisco Internetwork Troubleshooting Support (CIT). You must also agree to the Cisco Career Certifications and Confidentiality Agreement. Alternatively you can elect to take the composite exam. You must recertify every three years. CCNP and/or CCDP titles can also be recertified either by passing the composite exam or by passing both the BSCI and BCMSN exams.

Skill Level: Intermediate

C007 Cisco Content Networking Specialist (CCNS)

Description

For individuals who wish to demonstrate expertise with Cisco content networking solutions, including knowledge of content edge delivery, content distribution and management, content switching, and content routing. Part of the Cisco Qualified Specialist program. You must hold Cisco CCDP or CCNP or CCIP certification. You must also pass Cisco Content Networking Specialist Exam. You must also sign the Cisco Career Certifications Agreement. You must recertify every two years by taking the current exams.

Skill Level: Intermediate

C008 Certified Cisco Systems Instructor (CCSI)

Description

This certification is for individuals who want to teach authorized Cisco courses. You must be employed or sponsored by a Cisco Learning Partner. You must have hands on technical experience in bridging and routing, switching, and/or WAN environments, plus at least a year of technical teaching experience. You must be sponsored by (or yourself become) a Cisco Training Partner. In addition to meeting those conditions, you must attend the course you wish to teach, and then pass the related exam.

Afterwards, you must attend and pass a two-day Instructor Certification Process (ICP) at Cisco. To extend the certification to additional courses, you'll have to attend the course, pass the related exam, and submit a request to extend their certification to include the new course. You must maintain 4.0 out of 5.0 on student critiques. You must maintain a relationship with a Cisco Training Partner or your certification lapses.

Skill Level: Advanced

C009 Cisco Certified Security Professional (CCSP)

Description

For individuals who wish to demonstrate expertise in designing and implementing Cisco secure networks. That includes designing end to end network security solutions using the Cisco SAFE blueprint, using Cisco devices and technologies to implement a defense strategy, and managing network security. You must already hold Cisco's CCNA certification, plus pass five additional exams as follows: Securing Networks with Cisco Routers and Switches; Securing Networks with PIX and ASA; Implementing Cisco Intrusion Prevention System; Securing Hosts Using Cisco Security Agent; Securing Cisco Network Devices. You must also sign the Cisco Career Certifications Agreement. You must recertify every three years by completing one of the following options: pass Cisco SAFE Implementation Exam, pass any CCIE written exam, or achieve the CCIE certification.

Skill Level: Advanced

C010 Cisco Optical Specialist (COP)

Description

For network professionals who design, install, operate, and maintain optical networking systems using Cisco products, part of the Cisco Qualified Specialist program. The exam covers SONET/SDH, DWDM, DPT/RPR, POS optical cross connects, Ethernet over optical, and element management, and other protocols and technologies relevant to optical networking using Cisco products. You must also sign the Cisco Career Certifications Agreement. You must recertify every two years by taking the then current exam.

Skill Level: Basic

4.2 CompTIA Certifications

CompTIA

The Computing Technology Industry Association (**CompTIA**) is the voice of the world's $3 trillion information technology industry. CompTIA membership extends into more than 100 countries and includes companies at the forefront of innovation; the channel partners and solution providers they rely on to bring their products to market; and the professionals responsible for maximizing the benefits organizations receive from their technology investments.

http://www.comptia.org

C011 A+

Description

This certification is for entry-level. This is a popular first certification, especially for individuals switching from another career to computers. You must pass two test modules-the Core and a WIN/DOS module.

Skill Level: Basic

C012 Certified Document Imaging Architects (CDIA+)

Description

Certified Document Imaging Architects (CDIA+) possess critical knowledge of all major areas and technologies used to plan, design and specify an imaging system. It is for system architects and designers, sales and sales support engineers, technical support professionals, technology evaluators and corporate buyers, system administrators, technology professionals and consultants. You must pass CDIA exam.

Skill Level: Basic

C013 Certified Technical Trainer (CTT+)

Description

CompTIA CTT+ Certification is a cross-industry credential recognizing excellent instructional abilities. A CTT+ certification demonstrate core competencies that include instructor knowledge and credibility, classroom performance, and effective communication and presentation skills. You must pass CTT+ exam.

Skill Level: Advanced

C014 e-Biz+

Description

For technical and non-technical individuals who work in an e-Business environment. It covers the business concepts of Supply Chain Management, Customer Relationship Management, Electronic Commerce and IT infrastructure. Originally was Gartner e-Business certification. You must pass e-Biz+ exam.

Skill Level: Intermediate

C015 HTI+

Description

HTI+ is for technicians who install and troubleshoot integrated residential subsystems. This includes the integration and distribution of multiple subsystems, including: Communications Network; Entertainment Network; Security Network; Home Control Network; Services and Subscription; Commercial Wiring/Cabling and Computer Network. HTI stands for Home Technology Integrator. You must pass two exams: Residential Subsystems and Systems Infrastructure and Integration.

Skill Level: Basic

C016 i-Net+

Description

i-Net+ is for individuals who are hands-on specialists responsible for implementing and maintaining Internet, Intranet and Extranet infrastructure and services as well as development of related applications. You must pass i-Net+ exam.

Skill Level: Basic

C017 Linux+

Description

This certification demonstrates foundation level Linux operating system proficiency. You must pass Linux+ exam.

Skill Level: Basic

C018 Network+

Description

This certification is for networking technicians with 18-24 months of experience. You must pass the Network+.

Skill Level: Intermediate

C019 Project+ (formerly IT Project+)

Description

For individuals who lead and manage projects. This used to be Information Technology specific. You must pass Project+ exam.

Skill Level: Intermediate

C020 Security+

Description

Security+ is for individuals who are foundation-level IT security workers. This vendor-neutral certification covers such topics as firewalls, viruses, user authentication and encryption. It requires passing a single exam. The exam covers general security concepts, communications security, basics of cryptography, and operational/organizational security.

Skill Level: Basic

C021 Server+

Description

Server+ is for individuals who wish to demonstrate expertise with advanced PC hardware issues such as RAID, SCSI, multiple CPUs, SANs and more. You must pass Server+ exam.

Skill Level: Intermediate

4.3 IBM Certifications

IBM is expressed in an ever-changing corporate culture, in transformational strategies, and in new and compelling offerings for customers. IBM's character has been formed over nearly 100 years of doing business in the field of information-handling. Nearly all of the company's products were designed and developed to record, process, communicate, store and retrieve information - from its first scales, tabulators and clocks to today's powerful computers and vast global networks.

IBM helped pioneer information technology over the years and it stands today at the forefront of a worldwide industry that is revolutionizing the way in which enterprises, organizations and people operate and thrive.

http://www.ibm.com

C022 IBM Certified Advanced Application Developer - Rational Application Developer for WebSphere Software

Description

This certification involves a stand-alone advanced level test. It is intended for developers with extensive experience developing enterprise applications using IBM Rational Application Developer for WebSphere Software. Earning this certification demonstrates the candidate has comprehensive knowledge of and can give expert advice to others related to IBM Rational Application Developer for WebSphere Software. The Advanced Application Developer uses IBM Rational Application Developer for WebSphere Software to design, create and maintain Java 2 Platform, Enterprise Edition (J2EE) applications, and to deploy and configure these applications. You must pass one test.

Skill Level: Advanced

C023 IBM Certified Advanced Database Administrator – DB2 Universal Database for Linux, UNIX, and Windows

Description

An IBM Certified Advanced Database Administrator is the lead DBA for the DB2 products on one or more of the following platforms: Linux, UNIX (including AIX, HP-UX, and Sun Solaris), and Windows. This individual has extensive experience as a DBA and extensive knowledge of DB2 Universal Database. You must pass three tests.

Skill Level: Advanced

C024 IBM Certified Advanced Deployment Professional - Tivoli Enterprise Management Solutions

Description

An IBM Certified Advanced Deployment Professional - Tivoli Enterprise Management Solutions is an individual who has demonstrated a higher level of implementation knowledge and skill both in breadth and in depth in the IBM Tivoli Enterprise Management solutions area. You must pass four required tests.

Skill Level: Advanced

C025 IBM Certified Advanced System Administrator - WebSphere Application Server

Description

This Certified Advanced System Administrator is an individual with extensive product knowledge, who is expected to perform all of the tasks of an IBM Certified System Administrator - WebSphere Application Server, Basic Administration. In addition, the Advanced System Administrator is expected to understand the complexities of infrastructure design and maintenance, analyze architecture and security issues, and perform advanced troubleshooting. An Advanced System Administrator is also expected to identify performance bottlenecks and provide administrative solutions where appropriate. You must pass one test.

Skill Level: Advanced

C026 IBM Certified Application Developer – DB2 Universal Database Family

Description

An IBM Certified Application Developer is an intermediate or advanced level application developer specializing in creating applications that run on any of the DB2 platforms: Linux, UNIX (including AIX, HP-UX, and Sun Solaris), and Windows, z/OS, s/390, and iSeries. This individual has strong skills in all common programming tasks as well as strong skills in one or more of the specialty areas: embedded SQL programming, ODBC/CLI programming or Java programming. You must pass two tests.

Skill Level: Intermediate/Advanced

C027 IBM Certified Application Developer - Rational Application Developer for WebSphere Software

Description

This certification involves a stand-alone intermediate level test. It is intended for developers with Web development experience using IBM Rational Application Developer for WebSphere Software. These Application Developers design, develop, debug, profile, and deploy J2EE Web applications and Java applications. The applications may include HTML, Servlets, Java Server Pages (JSPs) and EJBs. The applications may also make use of Web Services and JDBC technology. The Application Developer applies sound object-oriented analysis and design techniques and exhibits proficiency in the use of the Java language. You must pass one test.

Skill Level: Intermediate

C028 IBM Certified Associate Developer - Rational Application Developer for WebSphere Software

Description

This certification requires product knowledge and experience with IBM Rational Web Developer for WebSphere Software or IBM Rational Application Developer for WebSphere Software. This certification involves a stand-alone entry level test and is not a prerequisite for other IBM certifications. It is intended for new adopters of IBM Rational Web Developer or IBM Rational Application Developer for WebSphere Software, specifically professionals and students entering into Web development using IBM products.

Areas not covered as part of this certification because they are specifically addressed by other IBM certification offerings include Portal development, Web Services, EJB development, and XML tools. Additionally, Enterprise Generation Language (EGL) is not covered. The Associate Developer provides application development services related to design, implementation, testing, debugging, and deployment of J2EE Web applications and Java applications.

The applications typically make use of Servlets, JSPs, HTML, and JDBC technology. The Associate Developer applies object-oriented analysis and design techniques, makes proper use of the IBM Rational Web Developer or IBM Rational Application Developer for WebSphere Software products, and exhibits the ability to use the Java language to develop simple Web applications.

Skill Level: Basic

C029 IBM Certified Associate Developer - WebSphere Studio

Description

This certification is intended for new adopters of WebSphere Application Development technology, specifically professionals and students entering into Web Development using IBM products. Areas not covered include Web Services, EJB™ development, Team Tools and XML tooling. Other IBM certification offerings specifically address these areas. The Developer Associate is an individual with extensive product knowledge, who provides application development services related to design, implementation, debugging, and deployment of J2EE™ web applications and Java™ applications.

The applications typically make use of Servlets, Java Server Pages™ (JSP™), HTML, JavaBeans™, and JDBCTM technology. The Developer Associate is expected to apply object-oriented analysis and design techniques, make proper use of one of the IBM WebSphere Studio family of products, and exhibit the ability to use the Java language to develop simple web applications. This certification is a stand-alone entry level test and not a prerequisite for other IBM certifications.

This certification is appropriate if you have experience with IBM WebSphere Studio Site Developer, IBM WebSphere Studio Application Developer, IBM WebSphere Studio Application Developer Integration Edition, or IBM WebSphere Studio Enterprise Developer. You must pass one test.

Skill Level: Basic

C030 IBM Certified Database Administrator - DB2 UDB for Linux, UNIX and Windows

Description

If you are knowledgeable with DB2 Universal Database and are capable of performing the intermediate to advanced skills required in the day-to-day administration of DB2 instances and databases, you may benefit from this certification role. To attain this certification, you must either pass two tests or be certified as an IBM Certified Solutions Expert - DB2 Universal Database Administration for UNIX, Windows and OS/2 and pass one test.

Skill Level: Intermediate/Advanced

C031 IBM Certified Database Administrator - DB2 Universal Database for z/OS

Description

The IBM Certified Database Administrator is the lead database administrator (DBA) for the DB2 UDB product for the z/OS operating system. This individual has significant experience as a DBA and extensive knowledge of the DB2 Universal Database, specifically the new features and functionality related to. This specialist is capable of performing the intermediate to advanced tasks related to database design and implementation, operation and recovery, security and auditing, performance, and installation and migration specific to the z/OS operating system. To attain this certification, you must pass two tests or be certified as an IBM Certified Solutions Expert - DB2 Universal Database Administration for UNIX, Windows and OS/2 and pass Test 702.

Skill Level: Intermediate/Advanced

C032 IBM Certified Database Associate – DB2 Universal Database Family

Description

This Database Associate is an entry level DBA or a user of any of the DB2 family of products. This individual is knowledgeable about the fundamental concepts of DB2 Universal Database through either hands on experience or formal and informal education. The database associate should have an in-depth knowledge of the basic to intermediate tasks required in day-to-day administration, basic SQL (Structured Query Language), understand how DB2 Universal Database is packaged and installed, understand how to create databases and database objects, and have a basic knowledge of database security and transaction isolation. This certification is also applicable for DB2 UDB for iSeries. You must pass one test.

Skill Level: Basic

C033 IBM Certified Deployment Professional - IBM WebSphere Commerce

Description

This certification targets intermediate level deployment professionals. This deployment professional is an individual with extensive product knowledge, who primarily installs, configures, and maintains e-commerce sites using IBM WebSphere. This deployment professional has a general awareness of how the product components interact and the capabilities of the components, as well as customization options. This deployment professional can handle the following administrative tasks:

- Successfully install the product.
- Publish a sample starter store and verify that it is working.
- Set up and control user access to the site.
- Successfully configure WebSphere Commerce Payments.
- Successfully configure messaging transports.
- Load catalog data into WebSphere Commerce.
- Explain and demonstrate the features of the administrative tools.

- Perform troubleshooting, ongoing administration and maintenance tasks.

It can also handle business related tasks such as explain how to use WebSphere Commerce Accelerator to manage the business operations of the store, including generating reports, analyzing data, and implementing appropriate business decisions. You must pass one test.

Skill Level: Intermediate

C034 IBM Certified Deployment Professional - Tivoli Access Manager for e-business

Description

This certification is a technical professional responsible for incorporating the defined security requirements of an organization, designing an Access Manager for e-business solution, and installing, configuring, integrating, administering, troubleshooting and supporting that installation. You must pass one test.

Skill Level: Basic

C035 IBM Certified Deployment Professional - Tivoli Configuration Manager

Description

This certification is a technical professional responsible for planning, installation, configuration, operations, administration, and maintenance of an IBM Tivoli Configuration Manager solution. You must pass one test.

Skill Level: Basic

C036 IBM Certified Deployment Professional - Tivoli Data Warehouse

Description

This certification is a technical professional responsible for planning, installation, configuration, customization, administration, maintenance and troubleshooting of an IBM Tivoli Data Warehouse solution. You must pass one test.

Skill Level: Basic

C037 IBM Certified Deployment Professional - Tivoli Enterprise Console

Description

This certification is a person who plans the TEC architecture and integration into the environment, installs the TEC code, analyzes the client's environment for best practices event management, writes the appropriate rules and adapter configurations, understands how to test the rules and adapters, and places them into production. You must pass one test.

Skill Level: Basic

C038 IBM Certified Deployment Professional - Tivoli Federated Identity Manager

Description

This certification is a technical professional responsible for the planning, designing, customizing, testing, troubleshooting, and documenting of solutions for IBM Tivoli Federated Identity Manager. You must pass one test.

Skill Level: Basic

C039 IBM Certified Deployment Professional - Tivoli Provisioning Manager with Orchestration

Description

This certification is a technical professional responsible for the planning, installation, environment setup, configuration, testing and troubleshooting of the IBM Tivoli Provisioning Manager with Orchestration solution. You must pass one test.

Skill Level: Basic

C040 IBM Certified Deployment Professional - WebSphere InterChange Server and Toolset

Description

This certification ensures the success of WebSphere InterChange Server implementations as part of IBM's business integration solutions. The Certified Deployment Professional should have thorough product configuration/development knowledge and deploy best practices. This Deployment Professional is also expected to have hands-on experience with design and implementation of process integration solutions. The target audience for this certification includes Consultants, IT Specialists, and Architects. You must pass one test.

Skill Level: Intermediate

C041 IBM Certified Enterprise Developer - WebSphere Studio

Description

For the Web site designer and Webmasters who utilize WebSphere Application Server. This Enterprise Developer develops and deploys distributed enterprise-level applications that model an organization's processes, practices, and concepts. This is accomplished by designing, creating and maintaining Java 2 Platform, Enterprise Edition (J2EE) components, deploying and configuring these components, and supporting the development of application clients that access them.

This developer is an individual with extensive product knowledge, who works with business analysts, application architects, application assemblers, and administrators. He or she is expected to apply sound object-oriented analysis and design techniques during development. This developer understands application assembly within the business domain across a multi-tier architecture. This individual has the system administration skills required to tune the application to meet performance requirements.

Certification can be achieved if you have experience with IBM WebSphere Studio Application Developer, IBM WebSphere Studio Application Developer, Integration Edition, or IBM WebSphere Studio Enterprise Developer. Must hold Sun Java certification plus pass three additional exams. The additional exams cover UML, Enterprise connectivity with J2EE, and Enterprise application development with IBM WebSphere Studio.

Skill Level: Advanced

C042 IBM Certified Infrastructure Systems Architect

Description

This certification is designed to enhance the technical sales and solution design skills of an individual within the Business Partner firm to be better able to define and develop comprehensive client solutions. Comprehensive client solutions can generate greater financial results to the firm while clients can benefit by implementing leading-edge solutions that pay off faster. I-SA will develop and validate strong technical leadership skills enabling them to architect and design complex IT infrastructure solutions that include integrated multiple server platforms, software middleware, storage, and services. All of which can translate into increased customer satisfaction and loyalty.

Skill Level: General

C043 IBM Certified Instructor - IBM WebSphere Application Server Network Deployment, System Administration

Description

The system administration instructor is responsible for teaching course SW246, IBM WebSphere Application Server Administration. This course teaches students how to install, configure, and maintain IBM WebSphere Application Server "base" and Network Deployment, and to deploy enterprise Java applications in a single machine or clustered configuration.

Skill Level: General

C044 IBM Certified Instructor - IBM WebSphere Studio, Application Development

Description

The application development instructor is responsible for teaching the following courses:

1. **SW243 Introduction to Java using IBM WebSphere Studio Application Developer**

   It introduces the student to Java and to WebSphere Studio Application Developer simultaneously, and encourages him to use Application Developer as a guide to exploring Java.

2. **SW284 Servlet and JSP Development with IBM Rational Application Developer**

It is designed to introduce Java developers to the development and testing of server-side applications based on the J2EE component model, using IBM WebSphere and IBM Rational tools. Course topics include the development and testing of server-side applications that use Servlets and JSP technology for the control and flow of e-business applications, and use JavaBeans to represent the business logic, the development and use of custom tags for JSP, Servlets filters and listeners.

3. **SW237 Developing Web Applications with IBM WebSphere Studio Application Developer**

   It explores the Web application development features of IBM WebSphere Studio Application Developer. It provides an overview of the features in J2EE and its support within this version of WebSphere Studio. Lab exercises will strengthen your ability to use WebSphere Studio to create Servlets and JSP, incorporate database access and XML in your applications as well as debugging and profiling.

Skill Level: General

C045 IBM Certified Solution Designer - DB2 Business Intelligence

Description

If you are knowledgeable of IBM's Business Intelligence solutions and the fundamental concepts of DB2 Universal Database, and are capable of performing the intermediate and advanced skills required to design, develop and support Business Intelligence applications. This certification is applicable to those who specialize in identifying the business and technical requirements of a Business Intelligence opportunity; and consult, architect and manage Business Intelligence solutions. This is a software based test for use by consultants and implementers that is based on IBM's Business Intelligence software and solutions. You must pass two tests.

Skill Level: Intermediate/Advanced

C046 IBM Certified Solution Designer - DB2 Content Manager

Description

This certification has detailed technical knowledge about DB2 Content Manager. The certification candidate will be required to apply the concepts and have general knowledge about the DB2 Content Manager portfolio. This specialist performs the following tasks related to DB2 Content Manager: High-level design and requirements gathering; installation and configuration; troubleshooting; user and system administration; maintenance and performance tuning; and solution migration and integration.

This expert understands when DB2 Content Manager is the appropriate solution, and had the core competencies in installing, managing and installing Content Manager. This specialist has the knowledge of functions specific to the Content Manager Library Server, Resource Manager, System Administration, System Managed Storage, MS Windows client and Content Manager e-Client. You must pass one test.

Skill Level: Advanced

C047 IBM Certified Solution Designer - WebSphere Business Integration Message Broker

Description

This certification is an individual with extensive product knowledge, who performs the following tasks:

- Evaluates and communicates the ability of a WebSphere Business Integration Message Broker based solution to solve a given business problem.
- Gathers requirements and architects an integrated WebSphere Business Integration Message Broker based solution.
- Defines run time architecture.
- Identifies or designs message sets/formats.
- Designs message flows.
- Plans and implements a proof of concept for the critical points of a solution.

The target audience for this certification includes Consultants, Technical Specialists and Architects. You must pass two tests.

Skill Level: Intermediate

C048 IBM Certified Solution Designer - WebSphere MQ

Description

An IBM Certified Solution Designer - WebSphere MQ is an individual with extensive product knowledge, who performs the following tasks:

- Understands the basic concepts of asynchronous messaging and WebSphere MQ.
- Plans and architects software solutions involving WebSphere MQ.
- Designs applications based on WebSphere MQ and demonstrates knowledge and experience in a wide variety of WebSphere MQ platforms and versions/releases sets/formats.

Related aspects of the solution:

- Code reviews, Data compression, Deployment, Exits, Message standards.
- Naming Standards, Protocols, Recovery, Performance, Availability, Scalability, Security.
- Systems Administration, Prototyping, Testing, Triggering, Use of related products.

You must pass one test.

Skill Level: Intermediate

C049 IBM Certified Solution Designer - WebSphere MQ Workflow

Description

An IBM Certified Solution Designer - WebSphere MQ Workflow is an individual with extensive product knowledge, who maps Business Process Requirements into an overall WebSphere MQ Workflow solution for business integration. The Solution Designer is expected to perform the following tasks:

- Consult on WebSphere MQ Workflow implementation options.
- Create complete business process definitions for execution by WebSphere MQ Workflow (using WebSphere MQ Workflow Buildtime or WebSphere Business Integration Modeler).
- Consult on various integration capabilities and end user interfaces including programming interfaces, integration to backend systems, authentication systems, and databases.
- Map WebSphere MQ Workflow solutions to integration architectures.
- Construct Runtime environment by setting up and configuring WebSphere MQ Workflow.
- Test the WebSphere MQ Workflow model for completeness.

The target audience for this certification includes Consultants, Technical Specialists and Architects. You must pass one test.

Skill Level: General

C050 IBM Certified Solution Developer - IBM WebSphere Portal

Description

This certification targets intermediate level J2EE developers, architects or consultant with extensive product knowledge who design or develop portal solutions. These individuals have a breadth of basic operational services skills in more than one environment and with both the Express and Multiplatform offerings, and a full foundation in Enable Edition. This solution developer can:

- Program and design portal solutions using IBM WebSphere Portal.
- Develop, test, debug, deploy, and configure portlets as part of a larger portal base solution.
- Understand the portal test environment within WebSphere Studio to configure and deploy a test portal to aid debugging portlets and portlet applications.

You must pass one test.

Skill Level: Intermediate

C051 IBM Certified Solution Developer - Web Services Development with WebSphere Studio

Description

The Web Services Solution Developer is responsible for using WebSphere Studio Application Developer to design, create, package, publish, and test Web services, and support the development of clients that access them securely. The Solution Developer is an individual with extensive product knowledge, who is expected to apply sound Service Oriented Architecture (SOA) analysis and design techniques, using WebSphere Studio Application Developer.

This certification does not cover Web application development, EJB™ development, and XML tooling. This certification targets intermediate level developers who have experience in Web Services development and one or all of the following products:

- WebSphere Studio Application Developer.
- WebSphere Studio Application Developer Integration.
- WebSphere Studio Enterprise Developer.

You must pass one test.

Skill Level: Intermediate

C052 IBM Certified Solution Developer - WebSphere IIS DataStage Enterprise

Description

This certification has the critical knowledge and skills necessary to professionally design and develop an efficient and scalable DataStage EE solution to a complex enterprise level business problem; configure a scalable parallel environment including clustered and distributed configurations; collect, report on, and resolve issues identified through key application performance indicators; be proficient in extending the capabilities of the parallel framework using the provided APIs (buildops, wrappers, and components).

The qualified individual can design and develop a scalable complex solution using a minimum number of components, can precisely control data partitioning and provide for minimum data skew. This individual should also be able to configure a distributed or nonsymmetric environment and should be able to tune a parallel application to determine where bottlenecks exist and how to eliminate them.

The certified individual can work with complex data import and export scenarios (arrays, structures, tagged, packed, binary data, etc) and understands the intricacies of designing parallel solutions without relying on automated insertion of partitioning and sort operations. The candidate clearly understands what an inserted buffer operation is, can enable environment variables to collect performance statistics and can determine the appropriate response to the collected data. You must pass one test.

Skill Level: General

C053 IBM Certified Solution Developer - WebSphere MQ

Description

This certification is an individual with extensive product knowledge, who performs the following tasks: designs WebSphere MQ applications based upon high level architectural designs; develops WebSphere MQ applications and exits; and tests and debugs WebSphere MQ applications and exits. This Certified Solution Developer is expected to recognize platform differences and implement across multiple platforms. You must pass one test.

Skill Level: Intermediate

C054 IBM Certified Solution Developer - WebSphere Portal

Description

This certification targets intermediate level J2EE developers, architects or consultants with extensive product knowledge, who design or develop portal solutions. These individuals have a breadth of knowledge in basic operational services and skills for IBM WebSphere Portal Enable and can:

- Program and design portal solutions using IBM WebSphere Portal.
- Develop, test, debug, deploy, and configure portlets based on JSR 168 and the IBM provided extensions plus other applicable JAVA standards for portlet development.
- Understand portal development, portlet development, and debugging using IBM Rational Application Developer (RAD).

You must pass one test.

Skill Level: Intermediate

C055 IBM Certified Solution Developer - WebSphere Studio

Description

This Solution Developer is an individual with extensive product knowledge, who provides services related to designing, developing, debugging, profiling, assembling and deploying of J2EE™ Web applications and Java™ applications. The applications may include Servlets, JSP™, and HTML. The applications also typically make use of JavaBeans™ and JDBC™ technology. The Solution Developer is expected to apply sound object-oriented analysis and design techniques, make proper use of IBM WebSphere Studio, and exhibit proficiency in the use of the Java language itself.

Certification can be achieved if you have experience with IBM WebSphere Studio Site Developer, IBM WebSphere Studio Application Developer, IBM WebSphere Studio Application Developer, Integration, WebSphere Application Server-Express, or IBM WebSphere Studio Enterprise Developer. You must pass two tests.

Skill Level: Intermediate

C056 IBM Certified Solution Developer - XML and Related Technologies

Description

This Developer can design and implement applications that make use of XML and related technologies such as XML Schema, XSLT and XPath. He has a strong understanding of XML fundamentals; knowledge of XML concepts and related technologies; understands how data relates to XML, in particular with issues associated to information modeling, XML processing, XML rendering and Web Services; has a thorough knowledge of core XML related W3C recommendations; and is familiar with well-known, best practices. You must pass one test.

Skill Level: General

C057 IBM Certified Solution Expert - U2 Family Application Development

Description

This Developer provides application development services related to design, implementation, debugging, profiling and deployment of U2 software applications. Developers are expected to apply sound programming techniques and solutions common to both UniData and UniVerse database programming languages utilizing applicable API's available to produce robust applications. The applications may include SQL connectivity commands and techniques suitable for external use of U2 database data. Certification can be achieved if you have experience with designing an application for the UniData and/or UniVerse database and programming experience in either UniData or UniVerse programming language. You must pass one test.

Skill Level: General

C058 IBM Certified Solutions Expert - DB2 Content Manager OnDemand iSeries

Description

This certification has detailed technical knowledge about DB2 Content Manager OnDemand, applies these concepts and has general knowledge about the DB2 Content Manager family of products. There are two distinct specialties within this Certified Solutions Expert designation -- one for OnDemand for Multiplatform and another specifically for OnDemand for DB2 @ **server** iSeries.

This certification performs the following tasks related to DB2 Content Manager OnDemand: High-level design and requirements gathering; installation and configuration; user and system administration; initial system load; troubleshooting; maintenance; and Web enablement kit installation and configuration. In addition to having the above skills, the IBM Certified Solutions Expert - DB2 Content Manager OnDemand iSeries also conducts performance tuning as necessary on the iSeries platform. You must pass one test.

Skill Level: General

C059 IBM Certified Solutions Expert - DB2 Content Manager OnDemand Multi-platform

Description

This certification has detailed technical knowledge about DB2 Content Manager OnDemand, applies these concepts, and has general knowledge about the DB2 Content Manager family of products. There are two distinct specialties within this Certified Solutions Expert designation - one for OnDemand for Multiplatform and another specifically for OnDemand for DB2 @server iSeries. This certification performs the following tasks related to DB2 Content Manager OnDemand: High-level design and requirements gathering; installation and configuration; user and system administration; initial system load; troubleshooting; maintenance; and web enablement kit installation and configuration. You must pass one test.

Skill Level: General

C060 IBM Certified Solutions Expert - DB2 UDB Database Administration for OS/390

Description

If you are knowledgeable with DB2 Universal Database and you are capable of performing the intermediate to advanced skills required in the day-to-day administration of DB2 instances and databases. You must pass two tests.

Skill Level: Intermediate/Advanced

C061 IBM Certified Solutions Expert - DB2 UDB Database Administration for UNIX, Linux, Windows and OS/2

Description

If you are knowledgeable with DB2 Universal Database and you are capable of performing the intermediate to advanced skills required in the day-to-day administration of DB2 instances and databases. You must pass two tests.

Skill Level: Intermediate/Advanced

C062 IBM Certified Solutions Expert - DB2 UDB Family Application Development

Description

If you are knowledgeable with DB2 Universal Database and are capable of performing the intermediate to advanced skills required to design and develop DB2 Universal Database applications. You must pass two tests.

Skill Level: Intermediate/Advanced

C063 IBM Certified Solutions Expert - Informix 4GL Developer

Description

If you are a knowledgeable Informix 4GL Developer and are capable of performing the intermediate to advanced skills required to design and develop Informix database applications. You must pass one test.

Skill Level: Intermediate/Advanced

C064 IBM Certified Solutions Expert - Informix Dynamic Server System Administrator

Description

If you are knowledgeable with Informix Dynamic Server and you are capable of performing the intermediate to advanced skills required in the day-to-day administration of Informix databases. You must pass three tests.

Skill Level: Intermediate/Advanced

C065 IBM Certified Solutions Expert - Informix Dynamic Server System Administrator

Description

If you are knowledgeable with Informix Dynamic Server and you are capable of performing the intermediate to advanced skills required in the day-to-day administration of Informix databases. You must pass two tests, or be certified as a System Administrator for Informix Dynamic Server, and pass one test.

Skill Level: Intermediate/Advanced

C066 IBM Certified Solutions Expert - Red Brick Warehouse System Administrator

Description

If you are knowledgeable about Red Brick Warehouse and you are capable of performing the intermediate to advanced skills required in the day-to-day administration of a Red Brick Warehouse. You must pass one test.

Skill Level: Intermediate/Advanced

C067 IBM Certified Solutions Expert - U2 UniData Administration

Description

If you are knowledgeable with U2 UniData and you are capable of performing the intermediate to advanced skills required in the day-to-day administration of U2 databases. You must pass one test.

Skill Level: Intermediate/Advanced

C068 IBM Certified Solutions Expert - U2 UniVerse Administration

Description

If you are knowledgeable with U2 UniVerse and you are capable of performing the intermediate to advanced skills required in the day-to-day administration of U2 databases. You must pass one test.

Skill Level: Intermediate/Advanced

C069 IBM Certified Specialist - DB2 User

Description

This certification is designed for individuals who are knowledgeable about the fundamental concepts of DB2 Universal Database, through either hands on experience or formal or informal education. They should have an in-depth knowledge of the basic to intermediate tasks required in day-to-day administration, basic SQL, understand how DB2 Universal Database is packaged and installed, understand how to create databases and database objects, and have a basic knowledge of database security and transaction isolation. You must pass one test.

Skill Level: Basic/Intermediate

C070 IBM Certified Specialist - High End Tape Solutions

Description

This certification performs requirements analysis, architecture development/solution design, planning/installing, and post installation support for enterprise tape solutions. This specialist takes a consultative approach to support sales, and he or she trains customers and mentors peers in enterprise tape storage technical issues. This specialist has detailed technical knowledge about IBM high-end tape products, technologies, and solutions, as well as the skills to architect solutions to meet customer requirements. This specialist can describe in detail tape strategy and solutions, the storage industry, the competition, and business trends and directions. You must pass one test.

Skill Level: General

C071 IBM Certified Specialist - High-End Disk Solutions

Description

This certification performs requirements analysis, architecture development/solution design, planning/installing, and post-installation support for enterprise disk solutions. This specialist takes a consultative approach to support sales, and he or she trains customers and peers in enterprise disk storage technical issues. The IBM High-End Disk Solutions, Specialist has detailed technical knowledge about IBM high end disk products, technologies, and solutions, as well as the skills to integrate those products into customer solutions.

He or she can describe details for disk storage strategy and solutions, the storage industry, competition, and business trends and directions. This technical person has the ability to connect IBM TotalStorage high-end disk products to all IBM @**server** platforms and other supported operating systems and servers. You must pass one test.

Skill Level: General

C072 IBM Certified Specialist - @server i5 iSeries Domino Technical Solutions

Description
This certification evaluates a customer's iSeries and Domino needs to develop a Domino technical solution. This expert implements an integrated Domino iSeries solution and provides ongoing support to the customer. You must pass one test.

Skill Level: General

C073 IBM Certified Specialist - @server i5 iSeries Linux Technical Solutions

Description
This certification evaluates a customer's Linux and iSeries needs to develop a Linux technical solution. This expert assists in implementing this solution and provides ongoing customer support. You must pass one test.

Skill Level: General

C074 IBM Certified Specialist - @server i5 iSeries Multiple System Administrator

Description
The @**server** i5 iSeries Multiple System Administrator has two to three (or more) years of iSeries system administration experience and administers iSeries systems and environments that are more complex in nature than those that the administers. "Complex" systems can mean environments with multiple physical and/or logical systems. The purpose of this certification is to validate that Business Partners, customers, and IBMers have the detailed understanding and skill required to:

- Effectively administer iSeries in a multiple system environment.
- Run iSeries in a multiple system environment securely and as efficiently as possible.

You must pass two tests.

Skill Level: General

C075 IBM Certified Specialist - @server i5 iSeries RPG ILE Programmer

Description
The IBM Certified Specialist - @**server** i5 iSeries RPG ILE Programmer designs and programs RPG IV with ILE applications. This certification has a broad knowledge of RPG, and has the ability to provide guidance to others who program applications with RPG.

This certification replaces two previous certifications:

- IBM Certified Specialist - AS/400 RPG IV Programmer.
- IBM Certified Specialist - AS/400 RPG IV Developer.

You must pass one test.

Skill Level: General

C076 IBM Certified Specialist - @server i5 iSeries Single System Administrator

Description

The @server i5 iSeries Single System Administrator has 12 to 18 months of iSeries system administration experience and administers iSeries systems and environments that are less complex in nature than those that the @server i5 iSeries Multiple System Administrator administers. The purpose of this certification is to validate that Business Partners, customers, and IBMers have the detailed understanding and skill required to:

- Effectively administer a single iSeries system.
- Run a single iSeries system securely and as efficiently as possible.

You must pass one test.

Skill Level: General

C077 IBM Certified Specialist - @server i5 iSeries Technical Solutions Designer

Description

This certification has substantial experience analyzing customer business needs, designing iSeries-based solutions, and planning the implementation of the solution. You must pass one test.

Skill Level: General

C078 IBM Certified Specialist - @server i5 iSeries Technical Solutions Implementer

Description

The IBM Certified Specialist – IBM @server iSeries Technical Solutions Implementer has 12 to 18 months (or more) experience installing, integrating, implementing, and supporting multiple generations of iSeries-based solutions. The certified specialist has iSeries functional experience and has installed four or more @server iSeries servers. The purpose of this certification exam is to help validate that IBM Business Partners, IBMers, and Customers have the detailed understanding and skill required to effectively install and implement business solutions on IBM @server i5 iSeries and plan for their ongoing support. You must pass one test.

Skill Level: General

C079 IBM Certified Specialist - @server i5 iSeries WebSphere Technical Solutions

Description

This certification evaluates a customer's WebSphere and iSeries needs to develop an integrated WebSphere technical solution. This expert assists in implementing this solution and provides ongoing customer support. You must pass one test.

Skill Level: General

C080 IBM Certified Specialist - @server i5 iSeries Windows Integration Technical Solutions

Description

This certification evaluates a customer's Windows and iSeries needs to develop a Windows Integration technical solution. This expert assists in implementing this solution and provides ongoing customer support. You must pass one test.

Skill Level: General

C081 IBM Certified Specialist - IBM Storage Sales

Description

This certification identifies opportunities for business and generates/qualifies demand using a consultative approach. This specialist determines business needs and requirements, effectively uses available tools and resources to design and sell storage solutions that meet the customer needs and requirements, and positions the solution to satisfy the customer's business needs. The Storage Sales Specialist has a broad knowledge of the features, functions and benefits of IBM storage solutions and the IBM storage portfolio, including disk, tape, storage management software, NAS, SAN and virtualization, as well as an understanding of competitive offerings. You must pass one test.

Skill Level: General

C082 IBM @server Certified Specialist - iSeries System Command Operations

Description

If you are knowledgeable in iSeries terminology and capable of performing basic to intermediate level skills for day to day operations of an iSeries using commands and menu screens, you can prove your skills with this test. You must pass one test.

Skill Level: Basic/Intermediate

C083 IBM Certified Specialist - Open Systems Storage Solutions

Description

This certification performs requirements analysis, architecture development/solution design, installing/planning, and post-sales support for open systems storage solutions. This specialist takes a consultative approach to support sales, as well as train customers and peers in storage technical issues. The IBM Open Systems Storage Solutions Specialist has a wide range of technical knowledge about open systems and mid-range storage products, and has the skills to integrate those products into customer solutions. This specialist understands and is able to explain tape, disk and storage networking products, as well as storage management software and strategy. He or she can describe networked storage strategy and solutions, the storage industry as well as the competition, business trends and directions. You must pass one test.

Skill Level: General

C084 IBM Certified Specialist - Storage Networking Solutions

Description

The purpose of this certification is to recognize technical professionals who can effectively design and implement IBM storage networking solutions. The certification covers a broad portfolio of IBM storage networking solutions, including products, technologies and offerings. This certification is designed for technical professionals who design and implement IBM storage networking solutions, including IBM Business Partners and IBM employees working in technical roles such as FTSS, ATS, and Techline.

This certification designs IBM storage networking solutions to achieve client business objectives. This professional performs technical requirements analysis, designs storage networking solutions, provides technical sales support, installs storage networking solutions, and provides post sales support, including validation that client business objectives have been met and transfer of knowledge to clients related to storage networking technical issues.

This specialist knows the IBM storage networking product family and the architectural differentiators related to NAS, SAN, iSCSI, and related protocols such as FCIP, iFCP, NDMP, and TCP/IP. He or she knows the technical capabilities and features of SAN switches and directors (including those from Brocade, Cisco, and McData), NAS products (including the N Series and its underlying software), iSCSI, and products that support extension of fiber channel over networks.

Understanding of tape and disk products, as well as virtualization and storage management is key to successful implementation of networked solutions. He or she understands networked storage characteristics relative to installed operating systems and application environments, knows storage networking protocols, and creates data replication and disaster recovery solutions from an architectural perspective, taking into account client requirements for distance, performance, cost, growth, and so forth. You must pass one test.

Skill Level: General

C085 IBM Certified Specialist - TotalStorage® Networking and Virtualization Architecture

Description

This certification designs IBM TotalStorage end-to-end storage networking solutions to meet customer needs. This individual provides comprehensive storage networking solutions that include servers, storage virtualization, storage networking, storage devices, management software, and services. This specialist has detailed knowledge of storage virtualization, storage networking technologies and the corresponding management software.

He or she has broad knowledge of IBM storage products and their features and functions. This individual can describe in detail storage networking and virtualization strategies and solutions, the industry, competition, and business trends and directions. This specialist performs requirements analysis, architecture development/solution design, planning/installation, and ongoing support for storage virtualization solutions. He or she takes a consultative approach to support sales. He or she mentors peers and transfers knowledge to customers in storage networking and virtualization technical issues. You must pass the TotalStorage Networking and Virtualization Architecture test.

Skill Level: General

C086 IBM Certified System Administrator - WebSphere Portal

Description

This system administrator is an intermediate level implementer, administrator or architect with extensive product knowledge, who designs and/or implements WebSphere Portal. This individual has a breadth of basic operational services skills in more than one environment and with both the Express and Multiplatform offerings. He or she has a full foundation in Enable Edition. This individual:

- Can plan, install and configure implementations of IBM WebSphere Portal.
- Can cover areas such as architecture, security, integration with LDAP or custom user registries, and connections to back-end applications.
- Will know about administering users and groups, administering portals and pages, and implementing themes and skins, via both graphical and command-line tools.

You must pass one test.

Skill Level: Intermediate

C087 IBM Certified System Administrator - WebSphere Application Server Network Deployment

Description

This intermediate level system administrator performs the installation, configuration and day-to-day tasks associated with ensuring the smooth and efficient operation of a WebSphere runtime environment. This includes product installation, configuration and deployment of J2EE applications, connecting to back-end resources and basic troubleshooting. You must pass one test.

Skill Level: Intermediate

C088 IBM Certified System Administrator - WebSphere Application Server

Description

This certification targets intermediate level system administrators. This Certified System Administrator is an individual with extensive product knowledge, who is expected to perform the installation, configuration and day-to-day tasks associated with ensuring the smooth and efficient operation of a WebSphere run-time environment. This includes product installation, configuration and deployment of J2EE applications, connecting to back-end resources and basic troubleshooting. You must pass one test.

Skill Level: Intermediate

C089 IBM Certified System Administrator - WebSphere Business Integration Message Broker

Description

This certification is an individual with extensive product knowledge, who performs the following tasks:

- Plans for the use of WebSphere Business Integration Message Broker.
- Installs and configures WebSphere Business Integration Message Broker.
- Administers, maintains, and deploys to WebSphere Business Integration Message Broker domains.
- Plans for the coexistence of, and the migration from WMQI to WebSphere Business Integration Message Broker domains.
- Performs basic problem determination.

The target audience for this certification includes Consultants, Technical Specialists and Architects. It is expected that this intermediate level System Administrator. You must pass two tests.

Skill Level: Intermediate

C090 Certified System Administrator - WebSphere MQ

Description

This certification is an individual with extensive product knowledge, who is expected to plan for the use of WebSphere MQ in relevant environments, install and configure WebSphere MQ, implement WebSphere MQ applications, set up distributed queuing with appropriate security, administer and operate a WebSphere MQ network including enforcing operation or organizational standards, perform basic problem determination, incorporate appropriate system extensions including clusters and SSL security. You must pass one test.

Skill Level: Intermediate

C091 IBM Certified System Administrator - WebSphere MQ

Description

This intermediate level system administrator is an individual with extensive product knowledge, who is expected to plan, install, and configure the product as well as implement applications, set up distributed queuing, enable appropriate security, administer and operate a queue manager network, enforce organizational and operational standards, perform basic problem determination, and implement clustering. Due to the various platforms supported by WebSphere MQ this certification is a cross platform certification. You must pass one test.

Skill Level: Intermediate

C092 IBM Certified System Administrator - WebSphere Portal

Description

This system administrator is an intermediate level implementer, administrator or architect with extensive product knowledge, who designs and/or implements WebSphere Portal. This individual has a breadth of basic operational services skills in more than one operating system platform in the Multiplatform offering. This individual:

- Plans, installs and configures implementations of IBM WebSphere Portal. Implements features of such as virtual portals, business process integration, and WSRP.
- Understands areas such as architecture, security, integration with LDAP or custom user registries, and connections to external applications.
- Administers users and groups, portlets and pages, and themes and skins, via both graphical and command-line tools.
- Understands options for content management and integration such as search, personalization, PDM and WCM.
- Understands options for collaboration and Collaboration Center.
- Understands and has working experience in relational databases.

You must pass one test.

Skill Level: Intermediate

C093 IBM Certified Systems Expert - @server i5 iSeries Domino 6 Solution Sales

Description

This certification evaluates the sales professional's ability to successfully sell Domino on iSeries. You must pass two tests.

Skill Level: Intermediate

C094 IBM Certified Systems Expert - @ server i5 iSeries Linux Solution Sales

Description

This certification evaluates the sales professional's ability to successfully sell Linux on iSeries. You must pass two tests.

Skill Level: Intermediate

C095 IBM Certified Systems Expert - @ server i5 iSeries LPAR Technical Solutions

Description

This certification evaluates the customer's LPAR needs to develop an LPAR technical solution. This expert will plan and implement an integral LPAR iSeries solution and provide ongoing support. You must pass two tests.

Skill Level: General

C096 IBM Certified Systems Expert - @ server i5 iSeries WebSphere Solution Sales

Description

This certification evaluates the sales professional's ability to successfully sell WebSphere on iSeries. You must pass two tests.

Skill Level: General

C097 IBM Certified Systems Expert - @ server i5 iSeries Windows Integration Solution Sales

Description

This certification evaluates the sales professional's ability to successfully sell Windows integration on iSeries. You must pass two tests.

Skill Level: General

4.4 ISC2 Certifications

(ISC)²® is the globally recognized *Gold Standard* for certifying information security professionals throughout their careers. It certified over 50,000 information security professionals in more than 120 countries. It was founded in 1989 by industry leaders.

(ISC)² issues the Certified Information Systems Security Professional (CISSP®) and related concentrations: Information Systems Security Architecture Professional (ISSAP®), Information Systems Security Management Professional (ISSMP®) and Information Systems Security Engineering Professional (ISSEP®); the Certification and Accreditation Professional (CAP®); and the Systems Security Certified Practitioner ((SSCP®) credentials to those meeting the necessary competency requirements. Several of (ISC)²'s credentials meet the stringent requirements of ANSI/ISO/IEC Standard 17024, a global benchmark for assessing and certifying personnel.

http://www.isc2.org

C098 Certified Information Systems Security Professional (CISSP)

Description

For experienced professionals in the computer security field who are responsible for developing the information security policies, standards, and procedures and managing their implementation across an organization.

Must have four years of direct work experience (or 3 years with a college degree or equivalent life experience or 2 years plus a bachelors or masters degree in information security from an approved school) in one or more of the ten test domains of the information systems security Common Body of Knowledge (CBK). You must also subscribe to the (ISC2) code of ethics, and pass the CISSP exam. Recertification is required at three year intervals by earning 120 Continuing Professional Education (CPE) credits.

Skill Level: Advanced

C099 System Security Certified Practitioner (SSCP)

Description

For individuals involved in network and systems security administration who are responsible for developing the information security policies, standards, and procedures and managing their implementation across various hardware and software programs in their organization. You must pass the SSCP Certification examination, in the areas of Access Controls, Administration, Audit and Monitoring, Risk, Response and Recovery, Cryptography, Data Communications, and Malicious Code/Malware.

Candidates must also subscribe to the (ISC2) Code of Ethics and have at least one year of cumulative work experience in one or more of the seven test domains in information systems security. Recertification is required every three years, with on-going requirements for maintaining your credentials in good standing.

Skill Level: Advanced

4.5 JRCERT Certifications

JRCERT promotes excellence in education and enhances quality and safety of patient care through the accreditation of educational programs. The only agency recognized by the United States Department of Education to accredit educational programs in radiography and radiation therapy, the JRCERT accredits educational programs in radiography and radiation therapy and in the related disciplines of magnetic resonance and medical dosimetry.

Programs accredited by the JRCERT must demonstrate that they are in substantial compliance with the relevant JRCERT accreditation standards: Standards for an Accredited Educational Program in Radiologic Sciences (radiography and radiation therapy), Standards for an Accredited Educational Program in Magnetic Resonance, or Standards for an Accredited Educational Program in Medical Dosimetry.

http://www.jrcert.org

C100 jCert Enterprise Developer (jCED)

Description

Candidates must have Certified Solution Developer status (jCert Level 2B certificate). Candidates must show competency in enterprise connectivity with Java technology and enterprise development with an application server. Candidates must pass the following two exams: Enterprise Connectivity with Java Technology (jCert Level 3A available from IBM or Oracle). jCert Level 3B exams are available from BEA Systems, Hewlett-Packard/Bluestone, IBM, Oracle, Sun or Sybase.

Skill Level: Advanced

C101 jCert Java Programmer (jCJP)

Description

Candidates must demonstrate skill in the Java™ programming language. Candidates must pass the following exam: Sun Certified Programmer for the Java Platform (jCert Level 1 available from Sun).

Skill Level: Basic

C102 jCert Solution Developer (jCSD)

Description

Candidates must have Sun Certified Programmer for Java Platform status (jCert Level 1 certificate). Candidates must show competency in application development for the Java platform and object-oriented analysis and design with UML. Candidates must pass the following two exams: Object-Oriented Analysis and Design with UML (jCert Level 2A available from IBM, Oracle or ProsoftTraining.com/CIW). jCert Level 2B exams available from Hewlett-Packard/Bluestone, IBM or Oracle.

Skill Level: Intermediate

4.6 Macromedia Certifications

Adobe Systems Incorporated is an American computer software company headquartered in San Jose, California, USA. Adobe was founded in December 1982. The company name Adobe comes from Adobe Creek, which ran behind the house of one of the company's founders. Adobe acquired its former competitor, Macromedia, in December 2005.

Adobe's products include:

- Technologies, such as Portable Document Format (PDF), PDF's predecessor PostScript, and Flash.
- Desktop software, such as Adobe Photoshop and Adobe Audition.
- Server software, such as Adobe ColdFusion and Adobe Live-Cycle.

http://www.adobe.com

http://www.macromedia.co.il

C103 Certified Dreamweaver MX Developer

Description

This certification represents a professional level of expertise in the activities that demonstrate an individual's competency as a Dreamweaver developer. A certified individual should thoroughly understand the Dreamweaver application, web page design, and web page authoring, and supporting technologies. You must pass a challenging exam. The skills and knowledge certified by this examination represent a professional level of expertise where a certified individual can:

- Identify requirements and strategies for website design.
- Develop, implement, test, deploy solutions, and maintain websites.

Skill Level: Advanced

C104 Certified ColdFusion MX Developer

Description

This Certification represents a professional level of expertise and demonstrates the competency of a ColdFusion MX developer. You must pass a challenging exam. The basic knowledge and skills required to pass this exam include:

- Two or more years experience with one or more programming languages.
- Experienced in the applied use of an enterprise level database server.
- One or more years of experience creating applications using ColdFusion.

Skill Level: Advanced

C105 Certified Macromedia Flash MX Designer

Description

This Certification represents a professional level of expertise and demonstrates the competency of a Flash designer. You must pass a challenging exam. The skills and knowledge certified by this examination represent a professional level of expertise where a certified individual can Identify important components of effective planning and implement visual design, motion design, optimization and publishing output in a complex Macromedia Flash application.

Skill Level: Advanced

C106 Certified Macromedia Flash MX Developer

Description

This certification is based upon the most critical job activities a Flash Developer performs. You must pass a challenging exam. The skills and knowledge certified by this examination represent a professional level of expertise.

Skill Level: Advanced

C107 Macromedia Web Design Certificate

Description

The Macromedia suite provides three powerful tools – Dreamweaver, Fireworks, and Flash. This certification will teach how these tools work differently and how they work together to create and manage Web sites. It is designed for anyone who wishes to learn to build web pages and sites using the Macromedia tools. It is ideal for both novice and advanced web designers.

Skill Level: Basic/Advanced

4.7 Microsoft Certifications

Microsoft Corporation or often just **MS** is an American multinational computer technology corporation with 79,000 employees in 102 countries. It develops, manufactures, licenses, and supports a wide range of software products for computing devices. Its best selling products are the Microsoft Windows operating system and the Microsoft Office suite of productivity software. Microsoft reorganized into seven core business groups in April 2002. Later, on September 20, 2005, Microsoft announced a rationalization of its original seven business groups into the three core divisions that exist today: the Windows Client, MSN and Server and Tool groups were merged into the Microsoft Platform Products and Services Division; the Information Worker and Microsoft Business Solutions groups were merged into the Microsoft Business Division; and the Mobile and Embedded Devices and Home and Entertainment groups were merged into the Microsoft Entertainment and Devices Division.

http://www.microsoft.com

C108 Microsoft Certified Application Developer (MCAD)

Description

This certification provides industry recognition for professional developers who build powerful applications using Microsoft Visual Studio .NET and Web services. You must pass three exams - two core and one elective. The core exams include a Web Services and Server Components Exam, plus your choice of either a Web Application Development exam or Windows Application Development Exam in the language of your choice. Exams are available with either a Visual Basic or C# focus. Available electives cover such topics as BizTalk Server, Microsoft SQL Server, and Microsoft Commerce Server. If one exam is retired you will need to pass the replacement exam.

Skill Level: Intermediate

C109 Microsoft Certified Architect Program (MCAP)

Description

This certification identifies top industry experts in IT Architecture. These architects can employ multiple technologies to solve business problems and provide business metrics and measurements to describe the success or failure of the projects they drive.

Skill Level: Advanced

C110 Microsoft Certified Database Administrator (MCDBA)

Description

Microsoft Certified Database Administrator (MCDBA) Demonstrate that you have the skills that are necessary to lead organizations in the successful design, implementation, and administration of Microsoft SQL Server databases with the credential. Database professionals using Microsoft SQL Server should consider the new Microsoft Certified Technology Specialist (MCTS) and Microsoft Certified Professional Developer (MCPD) credentials. You must pass three core exams and one elective exam.

The core exams include one SQL Server administration exam (either Administering Microsoft SQL Server or Installing, Configuring, and Administering Microsoft SQL Server Enterprise Edition) and one SQL Server design exam (either Designing and Implementing Databases with Microsoft SQL Server or Designing and Implementing Databases with Microsoft SQL Server Enterprise Edition), plus either a Windows 2000 exam (Installing, Configuring, and Administering Microsoft Windows 2000 Server) or a Windows Server 2003 exam (either Managing and Maintaining a Microsoft Windows Server 2003 Environment or Implementing, Managing, and Maintaining a Microsoft Windows Server 2003 Network Infrastructure).

Skill Level: Advanced

C111 Microsoft Certified Desktop Support Technician (MCDST)

Description

This certification will get you started in your IT career by ensuring you have the skills to successfully troubleshoot desktop environments running on the Microsoft Windows operating system. You must pass two exams: Supporting Users and Troubleshooting Microsoft Windows Desktop Operating Systems; and Supporting Users and Troubleshooting Applications on a Microsoft Windows Desktop Operating System Platform.

Skill Level: Basic

C112 Business Intelligence Developer (MCITP)

Description

Microsoft Certified IT Professional: (MCITP: Business Intelligence Developer) is the premier certification for business intelligence system designers and developers. This certification demonstrates that you can design solutions, data transformations, and reports. Business intelligence developers design and implement multi-dimensional database models (logical and physical), data marts, data warehousing, data transforms, data analytics, and reporting solutions. This includes programming and customizing servers that use Multidimensional Expressions (MDX), customer transforms, and custom reporting solutions. Business intelligence developers are typically employed by mid-sized to large-sized organizations.

Skill Level: General

C113 Database Administrator (MCITP)

Description

Microsoft Certified IT Professional: (MCITP: Database Administrator) is the premier certification for database server administrators. Database administrators install or configure Microsoft SQL Server and manage or maintain databases or multidimensional databases, user accounts, database availability, recovery, and reporting. They also design or implement security or server automation and monitor and troubleshoot SQL Server activity. Database administrators are typically employed by mid-size to large organizations.

Skill Level: General

C114 Database Developer (MCITP)

Description

Microsoft Certified IT Professional: (MCITP: Database Developer) is the premier certification for database designers and developers. This credential demonstrates that you can design a secure, stable, enterprise database solution by using Microsoft SQL Server. Database developers design and implement relational database models (logical and physical) and database storage objects. They also program servers by using user-defined functions, triggers, stored procedures, Transact-SQL, or the CLR. They retrieve or modify data using SQL queries or tune and optimize queries. Database developers are typically employed by mid-sized to large-sized organizations.

Skill Level: General

C115 Microsoft Certified Learning Consultant (MCLC)

Description

The Microsoft Certified Learning Consultant (MCLC) credential recognizes Microsoft Certified Trainers (MCTs) whose job roles have grown to include frequent consultative engagements with their customers. They are more than technology trainers—they diagnose current and desired business performance and design learning solutions to bridge the gap. The MCLC credential is a distinct differentiator that demonstrates expertise within the Microsoft training community and among customers. It validates experience in building a consultative relationship and recognizes skills in designing, developing, implementing, and evaluating customized learning solutions.

Skill Level: General

C116 Microsoft Certified Professional (MCP)

Description

For individuals who would like to demonstrate their expertise with a particular Microsoft product, including Windows, SQL Server, Exchange Server, FrontPage, Visual Basic, Visual FoxPro, Visual C, and .NET. You must pass any Microsoft exam. Excluded exams are: Networking Essentials and Microsoft Windows Accelerated Exam for MCP Certified on Microsoft Windows NT. If the exam is retired, you will need to pass the replacement exam.

Skill Level: Basic

C117 Microsoft Certified Professional Developer (MCPD)

Description

If you are developing .NET Framework applications that use Microsoft Visual Studio the new Microsoft Certified Technology Specialist (MCTS) and Microsoft Certified Professional Developer (MCPD) credentials provide a simpler and more targeted framework to showcase your technical skills in addition to the skills that are required for specific developer job roles. The Microsoft Certified Application Developer (MCAD) and Microsoft Certified Solution Developer (MCSD) credentials provide developers who use Microsoft Visual Studio .NET with industry recognition of their Microsoft .NET development skills and experience.

Skill Level: Basic

C118 Enterprise Applications Developer (MCPD)

Description

The Microsoft Certified Professional Developer: (MCPD: Enterprise Applications Developer) credential demonstrates that you have the comprehensive skills that are required to build n-tier solutions that target both Web and rich-client user experiences. Microsoft Skills Assessments for Microsoft Visual Studio and Microsoft ASP.NET help developers focus their exam preparation training and find learning resources to upgrade from Visual Studio .NET and ASP.NET.

Skill Level: Basic

C119 Web Developer (MCPD)

Description

The Microsoft Certified Professional Developer: (MCPD: Web Developer) certification demonstrates that you have the comprehensive skills that are required to build interactive, data-driven Web applications that use ASP.NET for both intranet and Internet uses. Microsoft Skills Assessments for Microsoft Visual Studio and Microsoft ASP.NET help developers focus their exam preparation training and find learning resources to upgrade from Visual Studio .NET and ASP.NET.

Skill Level: Basic

C120 Windows Developer (MCPD)

Description

The Microsoft Certified Professional Developer: (MCPD: Windows Developer) certification demonstrates that you have the comprehensive skills that are required to build rich client applications that target the Windows Forms platform using the Microsoft .NET Framework Microsoft Skills Assessments for Microsoft Visual Studio and Microsoft ASP.NET help developers focus their exam preparation training and find learning resources to upgrade from Visual Studio .NET and ASP.NET.

Skill Level: Basic

C121 Microsoft Certified Systems Administrator (MCSA)

Description

The Microsoft Certified Systems Administrator (MCSA) certification will advance your career by ensuring you have the skills to successfully manage and troubleshoot system environments running on the Microsoft Windows operating system.

- Messaging candidates on the Microsoft Windows Server track must pass three core exams and one messaging specialization exam.
- Messaging candidates on the Microsoft Windows track must pass three core exams and one messaging specialization exam.

- Security candidates on the Microsoft Windows Server track are required to pass three core exams and two security specialization exams.
- Security candidates on the Microsoft Windows track must pass three core exams and two security specialization exams.

The required exams depend on choice of track. If one of the exams is retired, you will need to pass the replacement exam.

Skill Level: Intermediate

C122 Microsoft Certified Solution Developer (MCSD)

Description

The Microsoft Certified Solution Developer (MCSD) for Microsoft .NET credential is the top-level certification for advanced developers who design and develop leading-edge enterprise solutions using Microsoft development tools and technologies as well as the Microsoft .NET Framework and Microsoft .NET Framework. Developers who use the Microsoft .NET Framework and Microsoft Visual Studio should consider the new Microsoft Certified Technology Specialist (MCTS) and Microsoft Certified Professional Developer (MCPD) credentials. You must pass four core exams plus one elective. The first core exam is Analyzing Requirements and Defining .NET Solution Architectures. For the next three you must first choose a language track (currently C# or Visual Basic). Then pass a .NET Web Application Development exam, a .NET Windows Application Development Exam, and the Developing XML Web Services and Sever Components Exam for that language. Electives cover such topics as SQL Server, BizTalk Server, Microsoft SQL Server, and Microsoft Commerce Server. If one of the exams is retired, you will need to pass the replacement exam.

Skill Level: Advanced

C123 Microsoft Certified Systems Engineer (MCSE)

Description

Earn the Microsoft Certified Systems Engineer (MCSE) certification and prove your expertise in designing and implementing the infrastructure for business solutions based on the Microsoft Windows platform and Microsoft Windows Server System.

- Messaging candidates on the Microsoft Windows Server track must pass six core exams and two messaging specialization exams.
- Messaging candidates on the Microsoft Windows track must pass five core exams and two messaging specialization exams.
- Security candidates on the Microsoft Windows Server track are required to pass five core exams and three security specialization exams.
- Security candidates on the Microsoft Windows track must pass four core exams and three security specialization exams.

The required exams depend on choice of track. If one of the exams is retired, you will need to pass the replacement exam.

Skill Level: Advanced

C124 Microsoft Certified Trainer (MCT)

Description

For individuals who want to be qualified instructionally and certified technically by Microsoft to deliver Microsoft Official Curriculum instructor-led courses for Microsoft Certified Technical Education Centers (CTECs) and Microsoft Authorized Academic Training Program (ATEC) institutions. You must earn a Microsoft certification (MCSE, MCDBA, MCSD, MCDST, or MCP on particular exams) or a Microsoft Business Solution (MBS) certification.

You must also demonstrate your skills as a trainer. If you are a new trainer, provide proof that you have attended an instructional presentation skills or train-the-trainer course that has been pre-approved by Microsoft. If you are an experienced trainer, you can instead present an instructor certificate from Caldera, Certified Internet Webmaster, Cisco Systems, Citrix, Lotus, Novell, Oracle, Santa Cruz Operations, or CompTIA's CTT+. You must complete the MCT application.

Skill Level: Advanced

C125 .NET Framework Distributed Applications (MCTS)

Description

The Technology Specialist certifications enable professionals to target specific technologies and distinguish themselves by demonstrating in-depth knowledge and expertise in their specialized technologies. Developers holding the (MCTS: .NET Framework Distributed Applications) certification have demonstrated breadth and depth of skills and knowledge of Web services, .NET Framework remoting, Enterprise Services, and Message Queuing technology. Technology Specialists typically pursue careers as Web developers, Microsoft Windows developers, or enterprise software developers.

They may also be database developers and systems administrators who do not work with the .NET Framework daily but who want to show their breadth of technology experience. Microsoft Skills Assessments for Microsoft Visual Studio and Microsoft ASP.NET will help you focus your exam preparation training and help you find the learning resources that you need to upgrade from Visual Studio .NET and ASP.NET.

Skill Level: General

C126 .NET Framework Web Applications (MCTS)

Description

The Technology Specialist certifications let professionals target specific technologies and distinguish themselves by demonstrating in-depth knowledge and expertise in their subject area technologies. Developers holding the (MCTS: .NET Framework Web Applications) certification have demonstrated breadth and depth of skills and knowledge of Web application technology and data access in Web applications. Technology Specialists typically pursue careers as Web developers, Windows developers, or enterprise applications developers. They may also be database developers or systems administrators who do not work daily with the .NET Framework but who want to show their technology experience.

Microsoft Skills Assessments for Visual Studio and Microsoft ASP.NET help developers to focus their exam preparation training and to find learning resources so that they can upgrade from Visual Studio .NET and ASP.NET.

Skill Level: General

C127 .NET Framework Windows Applications (MCTS)

Description

The Technology Specialist certifications enable professionals to target specific technologies and distinguish themselves by demonstrating in-depth knowledge and expertise in their specialized technologies. Developers who hold the (MCTS: .NET Framework Windows Applications) certification have demonstrated breadth and depth of skills and knowledge of Windows Forms technology, in addition to expertise in data access in Microsoft Windows applications. Technology Specialists typically pursue careers as Web developers, Windows developers, or enterprise software developers.

They may also be developers and system administrators who do not work with the .NET Framework daily but who want to show their breadth of technology experience. Microsoft Skills Assessments for Microsoft Visual Studio and Microsoft ASP.NET will help you focus your exam preparation training, and they can help you find the learning resources that you need to upgrade from Visual Studio .NET and ASP.NET.

Skill Level: General

C128 BizTalk Server (MCTS)

Description

The Technology Specialist certifications enable professionals to target specific technologies and to distinguish themselves by demonstrating in-depth knowledge and expertise in their specialized technologies. (MCTS: BizTalk Server) possesses a deep and broad understanding of the design and development of distributed applications that use BizTalk Server. The credential holder has also demonstrated expertise in deploying and managing a BizTalk Server solution and can create a BizTalk orchestration, integrate business rules and human workflow services, manage business processes, troubleshoot BizTalk solutions, and consume and publish Web services.

Skill Level: General

C129 SQL Server (MCTS)

Description

The Technology Specialist certifications enable professionals to target specific technologies and distinguish themselves by demonstrating in-depth knowledge and expertise in their specialized technologies. (MCTS: SQL Server) implement and maintain databases using specific instructions and specifications. They have thorough knowledge of the product, understand how to use the tools and Transact-SQL language, and know how to explore the user interface. Technology Specialists typically pursue careers as database administrators, database developers, or business intelligence developers.

Microsoft Skills Assessments for SQL Server help database administrators, database developers, and business intelligence developers focus their exam preparation training and find learning resources.

Skill Level: General

C130 Microsoft Office Specialist (MOS)

Description

Microsoft Office Specialist (Office Specialist) certification, the premier Microsoft desktop certification, is a globally recognized standard for demonstrating desktop skills. The Office Specialist program is helping meet the demand for qualified and knowledgeable people in the modern workplace.

Skill Level: General

4.8 Novell Certifications

Novell Data Systems began life in 1979 as a computer manufacturer and maker of disk operating systems. In January 1983, this company was renamed to Novell Inc. with the new target to develop and commercialize software and hardware for use in networks. The operating system NetWare was for the first time introduced in 1983. Novell developed his own network protocol IPX/SPX.

Novell purchased the company Ximian in August 2003 which one provided a Linux distribution of the same name and has developed the open source software Mono and Red Carpet. Ximian was founded in 1999. In April 2003 Novell published the plan also to provide all Netware services for Linux with complete technical support worldwide. Novell published in March 2005 the message that 75% of the company computers have been switched over to Linux and Open Office till now.

http://www.novell.com

C131 Certified Novell Administrator (CAN)

Description

CAN is for individuals who handle the day-to-day administration of an installed Novell networking product, and provide direct support to users. Requirements starting with NetWare 6: Must pass Foundations of Novell Networking exam. For NetWare 5: Must pass NetWare 5.1 Administration exam. As announced by Novell, from time to time. Usually tied to major product version releases.

Skill Level: Basic

C132 Certified Directory Engineer (CDE)

Description

CDE is for senior engineers and consultants involved in the design, implementation, optimization and maintenance of directories and directory-enabled solutions. You must hold either (Novell CNE), (Compaq ASE), (Microsoft MCSE), (IBM Certified Specialist), or (Cisco CCIE), before beginning. Then you must pass 3 additional certification tests: Directory Technologies written exam; Advanced NDS Tools & Diagnostics written exam; and a remote dial-up practicum. You must also submit an application to Novell. Recertification is required annually.

Skill Level: Advanced

C133 Certified Novell Engineer (CNE)

Description

CNE is for individuals who handle the day to day administration of Novell products, including Netware. You must hold NetWare CAN. You must pass 4 additional exams: Novell Network Management; Advanced Novell Network Management, eDirectory Design & Implementation, and Managing Desktops with ZENworks. There are alternatives to some of these exams. You must also agree to Novell's certification agreement. CNEs must periodically meet Continuing Certification Requirements (CCRs).

Skill Level: Intermediate

C134 Certified Novell Instructor (CNI)

Description

For individuals who want to teach Novell curriculums. You must hold current CNE or Novell CLP or Novell CLE. You must also hold a third part trainer certification such as CTT+, CCSI, CCI, HPCT, MCT or IPE. You must then complete the CNI intent form, and sign the Novell certification agreement. Annual renewal required.

Skill Level: Advanced

C135 Master Certified Novell Engineer (MCNE)

Description

MCNE is for individuals who provide solutions to complex networking problems that may span across several different platforms. It Focused on Novell products. You must hold a CNE on Netware 6, and hold CompTIA IT Project+ certification. In addition you must pass Novell's TCP/IP for Networking Professionals exam, plus pass two additional Novell electives. The electives include: Groupwise 6 Administration; Internet Security Management with Border Manager Enterprise; and Desktop Management with ZENworks for Desktops. Master CNEs must meet periodic Continuing Certification Requirements (CCRs). CCR information is available in CNE Net and will also be announced via Certification Headline News.

Skill Level: Advanced

C136 Master Certified Novell Instructor (MCNI)

Description

MCNI is for very experienced instructors who wish to teach Novell courses. You must be an MCNE. You must be a CNI before you can become an MCNI. You must pass exams at the instructor level that you want to teach. You must complete annual update requirement, chosen from a list of options. Options include such choices as attending a Novell conference or workshop, adding another certification from a specified list.

Skill Level: Advanced

C137 Novell Specialist (NS)

Description

For individuals who implement Novell products. You must pass one test verifying specific skills on Novell products. Courses offered are GroupWise Administration, Internet Security Mgmt w/BorderManager, TCP/IP for Networking Professionals, Desktop Management with ZENworks for Desktops, Integrating Novell eDirectory with Windows NT, Integrating Novell eDirectory and Active Directory, and Directory and Database Integration Using DirXML.

Skill Level: Basic

4.9 Oracle Certifications

ORACLE

Oracle Corporation is the world's leading supplier of software for information management, and the world's second largest independent software company. The company offers its database, tools and application products, along with related consulting, education, and support services.

Oracle is the first software company to develop and deploy 100 percent internet-enabled enterprise software across its entire product line: database, server, enterprise business applications, and application development and decision support tools. Oracle is the only company capable of implementing complete global e-business solutions that extend from front office customer relationship management to back office operational applications to platform infrastructure. Oracle software runs on PCs, workstations, minicomputers, mainframes and massively parallel computers, as well as on personal digital assistants and set-top devices.

http://www.oracle.com

C138 Oracle Database Administrator Certified Associate (OCA)

Description
OCA is an entry-level certification for individuals who work with Oracle database products. The first, Introduction to Oracle: SQL can be taken via the Internet or at a proctored testing center. The second, Oracle Database Fundamentals, is taken at a proctored test center.

Skill Level: Basic

C139 Oracle Database Administrator Certified Master (OCM)

Description
For individuals who wish to demonstrate advanced expertise with Oracle. This is the highest level Oracle certification. You must first become and Oracle Certified Professional. Then you must attend two advanced Oracle classes within your chosen technology role. Third, you must pass a two-day hands-on practical exam at an Oracle education facility. Finally, you must submit a Master Certificate Request form to receive your certificate.

Skill Level: Advanced

C140 Oracle Database Administrator Certified Professional (OCP)

Description
OCP is for Oracle DBA. You must first earn the Oracle Certified Associate (OCA) credential on your desired track. You must then pass the OCP DBA. You must then pass: Oracle Database: Fundamentals and Oracle Database: Performance Tuning.

Skill Level: Intermediate

C141 Oracle Internet Applications Developer Certified Professional (OCP)

Description
OCP is for Internet application developers using Oracle Forms Developer. who have completed training in their job role and have at least six months of experience. Must pass four exams: Introduction to Oracle: SQL and PL/SQL or Introduction to Oracle: SQL; Develop PL/SQL Program Units; and Build Internet Applications.

Skill Level: Intermediate

4.10 PMI Certifications

PMI (Project Management Institute) was founded in 1969 by five forward-thinking individuals who understood the value of networking, sharing process information and discussing common project problems. After their first official meeting at the Georgia Institute of Technology in Atlanta, Georgia, USA, the group officially incorporated the association in Newtown Square, Pennsylvania, USA.

PMI has grown to become the global advocate for the project management profession with nearly 260,000 individuals hold the Project Management Professional (PMP®) credential, making it the most widely recognized - and the only global - certification in the profession. PMI is actively engaged in advocacy for the profession, setting professional standards, conducting research and providing access to a wealth of information and resources. PMI also offers certification, networking and community involvement opportunities.

http://www.pmi.org

C142 CAPM™

Description

The Project Management Institute's Certified Associate in Project Management (CAPM™) certification covers: Initiation, Project Planning, Executing, Controlling, Close-out and Professionalism.

Skill Level: General

C143 CCR

Description

The PMI Continuing Certification Requirements Program (CCR), supports the ongoing professional development of PMI certified Project Management Professionals and the maintenance of PMP Certification. PMPs must accrue a minimum of sixty PDUs during each CCR cycle.

Skill Level: General

C144 PMBOK

Description

Project Management Body of Knowledge (PMBOK) is designed to give professionals the tools needed to successfully manage any type of project. This program enables you to manage your projects more efficiently and effectively. The curriculum covers in-depth the essential elements of initiating and completing a successful project, including the development of interpersonal skills to conduct work in the team environment inherent to modern projects.

Skill Level: Advanced

C145 PMI

Description

The Project Management Institute (PMI®) is project management's leading global professional association, and as such, it administers a globally accepted and recognized, rigorous, examination-based, professional certification program of the highest caliber. The PMI Certification Program maintains ISO certification in Quality Management Systems as evidence of its commitment to professional excellence.

Skill Level: General

4.11 RedHat Certifications

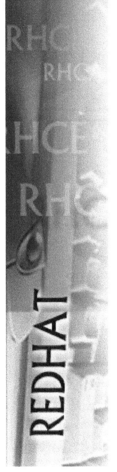

RedHat was founded in 1993. RedHat is the premier Linux and open source provider. Rated the number one enterprise software vendor for value in a *CIO Insight* Magazine study for four consecutive years, RedHat is the most recognized Linux brand in the world.

It serves global enterprises through technology and services made possible by the open source model. Solutions include RedHat Enterprise Linux, middleware, and a broad range of management and services: consulting, 24x7 support, RedHat Network. RedHat's global training program operates worldwide and features RHCE, the global standard Linux certification.

http://www.redhat.com

C146 RedHat Certified Architect (RHCA)

Description
RHCA is for individuals who wish to demonstrate advanced mastery of RedHat Linux. An RHCA has proven the skills required to plan, design and manage open source infrastructure in large complex environments consisting of many Linux systems across the enterprise. You must first hold RedHat's RHCE certification. Then you must pass five endorsement exams. The exams are: Security: Network Services; Deployment and Systems Management; Directory Services and Authentication; Storage Management; and System Monitoring and Performance Tuning.

Skill Level: Advanced

C147 RedHat Certified Engineer (RHCE)

Description
RHCE is for individuals who work with Linux and RedHat Linux in particular. This is a system administrator level certification. You must pass hands on lab exam. The closed-book exam consists of two elements: Troubleshooting and System Maintenance; and Installation and Configuration. You must complete all compulsory Troubleshooting and System Maintenance problems.

The lab exam is intended to verify that you can install and configure RedHat Linux; understand limitations of hardware; configure basic networking and file systems; configure the X Windowing System; configure basic security, set up common network (IP) services, carry out basic diagnostics and troubleshooting, and perform essential RedHat Linux system administration. To re-certify for a new release an individual needs to pass the RHCE Certification Lab Exam for the new release.

Skill Level: Advanced

C148 RedHat Certified Technician (RHCT)

Description
RHCT is for technicians who set up new RedHat Linux systems and attach them to networks. You must pass hands-on lab exam administered at RedHat facilities. The exam consists of two sections: a troubleshooting exercise, and installation and configuration exercise.

Skill Level: Intermediate

4.12 Sun Certifications

Sun Microsystems Inc. develops the technologies that power the global marketplace. Sun drives network participation through shared innovation, community development and open source leadership. It provides a diversity of software, systems, services, and microelectronics that power everything from consumer electronics, to developer tools and the world's most powerful datacenters.

Its core brands include the Java technology platform, the Solaris operating system, StorageTek and the UltraSPARC processor. It serves consumers and individual developers, alongside the largest global enterprises. It is network computing platforms are used by nearly every sector of society and industry.

http://www.sun.com

C149 Sun Certified Engineer for Sun ONE Directory Server

Description

It is for who design, deploy, configure, administer and troubleshoot. You must pass one exam: Sun Certified Engineer for Sun ONE Directory Server.

Skill Level: Basic

C150 Sun Certified Java Programmer

Description

It is for Java programmers. Certifications are available for several versions of Java 2 Standard Edition. You must pass Sun Certified Java Programmer exam for desired version.

Skill Level: Basic

CHAPTER

5 COMPUTER ADMINISTRATORS JOBS

Administrator is a person who manages and maintains a network of computers or a large multi-user computer. He is responsible for installing, configuring, and maintaining the networks and computers in the organization and to provide support in the development of customer websites and any Internet Services products or services that require programming and IT skills.

J001 Applications Administrator

Description
- Administer applications licensed from 3rd parties, such as Double-click Adserver, Siebel Email Marketing, version control, bug tracking, knowledge base, etc.
- Work with a team of DBAs and App Admin to support both technical and non-technical users of databases.
- Create and support reports.

Requirements
- BSc in Computer Science or Engineering.
- Perl/Shell scripting (JSP or ASP) and SQL (PL/SQL or t-SQL).
- Basic knowledge of http, SMTP protocols and Internet background.
- Good oral and written communication.

Recommended Certifications
C005, C016, C116, C129

J002 Contracts Administrator

Description
- Analyze proposals, preparing procurement file documentation and administering/managing subcontracts (processing modifications and task orders).
- Provide conflict resolution between company and subcontractors as it relates to contractual matters.
- Maintain small business award statistics and prepare reports for submittal to the government.
- Assist and provide training to program management to support procurement activities in support of prime contracts.

Requirements
- BSc/BA in Business related discipline.
- Experience administering Time and Material (T&M), Fixed Price and Cost type agreements. Experience administering working with GSA, GWACA, and IDIQ contracts.
- Experience in processing purchase orders in Deltek and processing procurement actions in compliance with the Contractor Purchasing System Review (CPSR).
- Willing to obtain CPM or other procurement certification.

Recommended Certifications
C012, C014

J003 Desktop Administrator/Systems Administrator

Description
- Resolve hardware and software problems expeditiously and with minimum disruption to computer system users and coordinates hardware repairs with vendors.

- Complete desktop related projects and Install personal computer related hardware and software according to schedule, scope of objectives, and standards.
- Assist with creating network user accounts and setting up user permissions for directories on servers.
- Administration of Active Directory and Group Policy settings and support of remote users.

Requirements

- Desktop support experience and expert in Windows administration and Microsoft Office.
- Experience with Active Directory administration including Group Policy and Exchange server administration.
- Excellent customer service skills and knowledge of industry standards.

Requirements (Desired)

- Experience with the following wired and wireless network technologies.
- Experience with OSX, RedHat, Linux, Network Appliance, Cisco IOS, PXE booting and Ghost.
- Experience with TPM management.

Recommended Certifications

C015, C018, C111, C148

J004 E-Mail Administrator

Description

- Provide system administrator for a large-scale UNIX-based messaging implementations.
- Hardware and system configuration, system monitoring and testing, site operations, routine system maintenance, traffic and performance monitoring.

Requirements

- TCP/IP, HPUX, SNMP and LDAP.
- Administration experience.

Recommended Certifications

C005

J005 Internal Systems Administrator

Description

- Monitor, analyze, and optimize existing infrastructure components to ensure continued operation including, but not limited to: Windows servers, Windows clients, Telephony systems, File and print services, Directory services and Intranet web site.
- Troubleshoot and resolve problems with infrastructure components to resume normal operations.
- Provide second level assistance to internally-generated trouble tickets and after-hours internal support on a rotating schedule.
- Ensure implementation of best practices for the management.

- Monitor and maintain the security and integrity of the technology-based assets.

Requirements

- BSc/BA degree or equivalent and MCSA certification.
- Experience with Windows-based network in an administrative capacity, Cisco-based networking infrastructures and networking technologies: DNS, DHCP, HTTP, LDAP, SMTP and SSL.
- Experience with Windows-based concepts: Active Directory, permissions and rights, Remote Installation Services, and Group Policy Objects, and Windows-based server and desktop platforms.
- Experience with MS Exchange, Word, Excel and PowerPoint.
- Strong attention to detail and ability to prioritize and multi-task.
- Ability to work independently on projects with minimal supervision.
- Excellent written, verbal communication skills and ability to travel.

Requirements (Desired)

- Microsoft Certified Systems Administrator – Messaging, Security.
- Cisco Certified Networking Associate/Professional.
- UNIX administration knowledge.
- IT Systems Administrator plus Programming Support.

Recommended Certifications

C003, C005, C019, C121, C130

J006 IT Systems Administrator

Description

- Maintain servers, software, network backup and documentation.
- Hand on desktop support, remote support and identify potential IT problems, as well manage and perform software/hardware improvements, upgrades and/or purchases.
- Administration of user accounts, files shares, file system, permissions and access rights.
- Oversee tech related projects, such as database design, development or implementation and desire to assist in developing databases using FileMaker and SQL.
- Ability and desire to assist in developing and working with other in maintaining Web pages and advising on how to help utilize the web to enhance the services to clients and Work with top management in developing an overall corporate IT strategy.

Requirements

- BSc Degree or equivalent experience.
- Knowledgeable in network systems, operating system and server applications, MS SQL, Symantec Anti Virus and FileMaker.
- FACSys, Avaya IP Office, Veritas Backup Exec, TCP/IP, DNS, WINS, DHCP, SMTP, Active Directory and Cisco PIX Firewall.
- Experience with Network administration, Microsoft operating systems and software, MS Exchange and MS Terminal Server.

- Able to perform system tasks such as back-up, upgrades, network troubleshooting.
- Experience in support and stand-alone network environment.

Requirements (Desired)

- Hand on MCSE and CCNA.

Recommended Certifications

C003, C005, C006, C018, C123, C129

J007 Lead System Administrator

Description

- Configure system and network parameters.
- Monitor system stability and performance.
- Help develop tools to monitor and maintain systems.
- Ensure 24x7 operations and occasional desktop support.
- Rapidly scale systems to meet demand.

Requirements

- BSc in Computer Science or equivalent.
- Experience with Linux or UNIX system administration.
- Knowledge of Apache, firewalls, load balancers and MySQL.

Recommended Certifications

C005, C017

J008 Linux Network & System Administrator

Description

- Maintain existing RedHat Fedora based UNIX servers along with network hardware and other supporting infrastructure.
- Keep UNIX pieces of telephone routing and billing infrastructure working, and proactive in detecting and fixing potential issues.
- Ability to plan, and implement expansion of the current infrastructure based on the business needs and requirements.
- Assist Linux developers in setting up their developer workstations, test frameworks for unit testing, performance testing, etc.

Requirements

- Strong Linux system administration skills.
- Strong knowledge of setting up LAN and WAN environments, routing, networking, DNS, DHCP.
- Hands on administration of Linux IP Chains/IP Tables firewall rules.
- Hands on knowledge of Asterisk IP-PBX, VoIP.
- Cisco IOS based routers support.
- MySQL database administration.
- Traditional Telco voice routing technologies.

Recommended Certifications

C003, C005, C006, C017, C147

J009 Linux Systems Administrator

Description

- Enhance, configure and support co-location web, SQL, monitoring servers and develop operational procedures.
- Identify, address, and document co-location infrastructural design flaws, procedures, and processes.
- Manage production site and venue data within the Reactrix web portal database, and deploy operating system, application software, and bug fixes via the Reactrix production web portal interface.
- Provide hardware, OS, and application maintenance on internal and production extranet Linux servers and Reactors, and deploy Nagios monitoring of servers and distributed Linux Reactors.
- Utilize Bugzilla to document and track troubleshooting opportunities and provide follow up/fixes to the production Reactor network.
- Enhance server and end user security through automated and procedural best practices. As well as conduct server security threat assessments and recommend/implement required modifications.
- Manage Jumpstart/Kickstart mechanisms for Linux servers and Linux end user desktops; as well maintain Veritas backup solutions across production and development Linux servers.
- Support VPN access to the corporate LAN from extranets and wireless DMZ locations, and utilize VPN tunnels for server-to-server administration and information optimization.
- Assure data integrity and restore-ability and archive data.

Requirements

- BSc or MSc in Computer Science, or equivalent.
- System/network administration experience in heterogeneous Linux RedHat Enterprise (RHEL) or CentOS and Windows environments.
- Experience in a networked production environment of Linux servers, server OS installation and maintenance in a production environment.
- Experience with installing and managing a web server application, and managing Linux services, startup scripts, networking, etc.
- Experience with installing scalable, thoroughly-monitored, stable IT servers, and application solutions.
- Ability to install software packages from source code and through the use of Linux package managers.
- Ability to implement, configure and manage data center and intranet Linux server systems.
- Working knowledge of at least one common scripting language (Perl, shell, etc).
- Capable of developing easily understood written documentation.
- Highly developed interpersonal and communication.

Requirements (Desired)

- Working knowledge of Apache, SAMBA, YP/NIS, DNS/DHCP, NFS filers, etc, and working knowledge of NAGIOS/NetSaint/SNMP.
- Working knowledge of intrusion detection systems, SQL database services, secure web servers, and web application load balancers.
- RedHat kickstart development skills.
- Cisco networking knowledge of switches, WAN routers and firewalls. As well as Linux/Solaris/Irix/operating system expertise.
- Prior experience working with a young startup.
- Security certifications.

Recommended Certifications

C003, C005, C006, C017, C018, C020, C121, C129, C148

J010 Network Administrator

Description

- Install, configure, and upgrade network hardware and software services, and maintain corporate intranet/external web presence.
- Resolve hardware and software related problems.
- Provide desktop and business application support.
- Perform system backups and recovery.
- Provide 24x7 support for system failures.
- Debug VPN connection issues, apply upgrades to NetApp filers, install and configure managed switches, and write rollout scripts for production websites.

Requirements

- BSc in Computer Science.
- Network administration experience with solid debugging and scripting skills.
- Administrating experience in Linux and Windows environments, as well as networking hardware.
- Knowledge of Exchange, Active Directory, RedHat, Apache, DNS, CVS, NIS, NetApp, and VPNs a plus.

Recommended Certifications

C003, C005, C006, C016, C017, C018, C021, C121, C148

J011 Network/Systems Administrator

Description

- Build out separate production, staging and maintain domain.
- Install fire walls, routers, load balancers and network monitoring.
- Establish backup routines/systems and upgrade existing hardware.
- Diagram and document entire infrastructure.
- Develop backup maintenance schedules.
- Set up new workstations.

Requirements

- BSc in Computer Science or similar degree.
- Experience with managing IT system and infrastructure.
- Ability to work cooperatively and proactively with staff inside and outside of the department and team player.

Recommended Certifications

C003, C005, C006, C016, C018

J012 NT/WEB Administrator

Description

- Install NT, Netscape enterprise servers, ColdFusion, Oracle, and SMS as well support NT/WEB Production Servers in a 24X7 environment using auditing, monitoring and diagnostic tools.
- Troubleshoot routers.

Requirements

- Experience with Netscape/NT Servers and LAN administration.
- Experience with IIS, SMS, Perl Scripting and ColdFusion.

Requirements (Desired)

- Experience with UNIX systems administration.
- Experience with Network engineering.

Recommended Certifications

C015, C016, C018, C104, C138

J013 Senior Database Administrator

Description

- Responsible for the administration of Oracle, Grid and ASM running on Sun UNIX or Linux operating systems.
- Able to implement databases on UNIX and Linux platforms.
- Create logical and physical database models/designs to meet the requirements of persistent data storage and retrieval.
- Responsible for performance tuning, security, software usage, capacity planning, training, recovery and backup procedures.
- Work with professionals in other disciplines to implement and integrate effective end user computer applications across multiple platforms.
- Propose project plans and designs to ensure projects are completed within time committed and budgeted.
- Research products and features and advises management concerning results of the research.

Requirements

- Oracle Certified Professional or equivalent.
- Experience in Oracle, ASM and Grid, TOAD, DB2 and SQL Server.

- Experience in a very high transaction rate OLTP applications.
- Working knowledge of Linux/UNIX operating systems, NT, MVS.

Requirements (Desired)

- Bachelor's degree.

Recommended Certifications

C017, C023, C110, C129, C138, C139, C140

J014 Senior Linux Systems Administrator

Description

- Care and maintenance the high-traffic Web servers.
- Monitor system stability and performance, and provide consultation and recommendation on computing solutions.
- Utilize a broad range of operating system, hardware, and software knowledge.
- Entail performing server and software upgrades and maintenance, as well as some internal customer service applications support.
- Enjoy working in a fast-paced environment where the support needs are everchanging.

Requirements

- BSc in Computer Science or related field.
- Experience with Linux and Windows servers administration.
- Experience in managing, maintaining and troubleshooting a co-located or managed Web server.
- Experience in building and maintaining SANs, EMC, cluster file systems, RedHat GFS.
- Experience with Samba, MySQL and SQL Server administration.
- Working knowledge of Apache, including vhost and mod_rewrite configuration, Shell, PHP and/or Perl scripting.
- Working knowledge of FreeBSD, Postfix and Nagios.

Recommended Certifications

C016, C017, C121, C129, C148

J015 Senior System Administrator

Description

- Organize and assign work assignments for team members on a project or day-to-day basis.
- Train and mentor team members on work procedures and use of software. As well as provide input for hiring decisions and performance evaluations of team members.
- Use knowledge of telecommunications, network and other systems environments.
- Install and operate systems, servers, PCs, laptops and other peripheral equipment in a Microsoft Active Directory environment.
- Prepare written reports, project plans and recommendations.

- Evaluate, coordinate, plan and implement software upgrades, using knowledge of business application software.
- Create and update operating procedure manuals.
- Support new technologies being tested and developed by the AOC with minimal formal training and support.
- Maintain and monitor communications between the AOC and outside agencies and vendors.
- Oversee the creation and maintenance of an inventory for computer equipment, user accounts, configurations, software releases and associated supplies.
- Analyze system performance and maximize efficiency.
- Organize, prioritize and coordinate multiple work activities.

Requirements

- Strong knowledge of Windows.
- Knowledge of Microsoft Office suite.
- Experience in Microsoft Active Directory environment.

Requirements (Desired)

- Ability to assess user requirements and implement creative solutions.
- Familiar with the following hardware: HP PC's and servers, Dell laptops/notebooks, Palm OS and Windows-based handhelds and HP printers.
- Familiarity with remote access solutions & web-based technologies.
- Working knowledge of Symantec Antivirus and backup software.

Recommended Certifications

C019, C020, C021, C099, C144

J016 Senior System/Network Administrator

Description

- Select and order hardware.
- Build and manage data to support an ASP model business.
- Design, configure and manage Network.
- Support general office infrastructure.

Requirements

- Experience with Linux and Solaris System Management.
- Experience with Oracle, Apache, Perl and shell scripting.
- Knowledge of Load balancers and other networking equipment.

Recommended Certifications

C007, C030, C145

J017 Senior UNIX Systems Administrator

Description

- Expand a world class network.
- Work with other team members to build Linux/BSD based systems.

- Work on a variety of tasks including system automation, configuration management, troubleshooting and maintaining high security standards within the network environment.

Requirements

- BSc in Computer Science or equivalent.
- Expertise in UNIX/Linux systems and TCP/IP Networking.
- Experience with Windows 2000+ domain administration, MySQL installation and configuration, and Email system (Qmail, Sendmail).
- Experience with a variety of H/W products (firewalls, routers, servers, etc) and Scripting.
- Excellent communication skills.

Recommended Certifications

C005, C017, C018, C020, C021, C121

J018 Senior Windows Administrator

Description

- Manage Windows systems that support email, file and print server, Active Directory infrastructure, as well as other Windows based infrastructure support.
- Manage Windows based software licensing automation, as well as design and rollout of automated software distribution tools.
- Support antivirus and anti-spam infrastructure, Windows Systems and infrastructure security both at the perimeter, and internally.
- Assist local and remote company staff with Windows Systems related problems.

Requirements

- Experience with Windows Server, MS Active Directory, MS Exchange and MS File and Print server technology.
- Experience in administration of wireless networking solutions.
- Strong ability managing Enterprise storage and backup technology.
- Familiarity managing MS SQL Server technology.
- Familiarity with Windows desktop support, application support, and Enterprise desktop management tools.
- Deep understanding of security technologies and remote access.
- Experience in setting up and maintaining secure VPN access (e.g. PPTP, IP-SEC, etc) and deep understanding of data integrity.
- Research and creative solution making ability.
- Experience with monitoring and notification systems.
- Ability to work individually and with a team and strong work ethic.

Requirements (Desired)

- MCSE certification.
- Constantly learn and improve upon oneself and the organization.

Recommended Certifications

C020, C111, C123, C129

J019 Solaris Administrator

Description
- Support large 24x7 Solaris/Oracle Production Web servers.
- Install SUN OS, Netscape enterprise server, compile open source code, automatic tasking with Perl scripts, build software source code distribution, and troubleshoot routers.

Requirements
- Experience with UNIX systems administration and TCP/IP.
- Experience with SUN/Solaris, Netscape server and Perl.

Requirements (Desired)
- Network engineering experience.
- Web administration experience.

Recommended Certifications
C017, C018, C149

J020 System Administrator

Description
- Maintain, evaluate and troubleshoot servers.
- Monitor the day-to-day operation of the servers, as well as but not limited to maintaining OS and related software.
- Monitor usage statistics, maintain system security server logs, modify configuration logs, and back up the systems, host builds.

Requirements
- BSc degree in computer technology or equivalent experience.
- Proficiency in Internet protocols and standards such as LDAP, SMTP, POP3, NNTP, Secure HTML, VPN, DNS, CVS and SVN.
- Experience with OSPF, BGP, Perl, PHP, AWK, SED, UNIX.
- Experience with firewall configuration and management.
- Strong understanding skills in security, networking, Internet, LAN and WAN technologies, and e-commerce technology.
- Experience working with Apache Web Server and databases, ODBC and MySQL.
- Ability to work independently and as part of a cross functional team and successfully handle multiple tasks.

Recommended Certifications
C001, C005, C014, C015, C016, C018, C020, C121

J021 Systems Administrator - Lotus Notes

Description
- Perform Lotus Notes account administration, including creation of Notes accounts, transition of existing Notes accounts for users, troubleshoot problems with Lotus Notes accesses, and suspend or delete Notes accounts as necessary.
- Provide second level customer support for Lotus Notes Client users and assist in maintenance of Lotus Domino servers. As well support enterprise-wide maintenance of servers and accounts.
- Support the customer's Windows servers and Lotus Notes mail and database servers, including regularly scheduled backups, installation and updating of application.

Requirements
- BSc in Computer Science or equivalent.
- Experience with Lotus Notes and Domino maintenance support.
- Strong knowledge of Windows, Lotus Notes server.
- Familiar with Networking fundamentals, including TCP/IP protocol, SMTP, DNS, DHCP, and WINS.
- Familiar with Microsoft Active Directory and Exchange environment.
- Strong communication and organizational skills.
- Able to work independently and as part of a cross functional team and successfully handle multiple tasks.

Requirements (Desired)
- Lotus Administrator CLP certified.
- Project management skills.
- Goodlink and BlackBerry Server Administration experience.
- Sametime Environment experience.

Recommended Certifications
C018, C021

J022 Systems Administrator/Gamer

Description
- Provide troubleshooting and administration work for all Studio applications and servers, including, but not limited to: File servers, Build servers, SAN, Marimba, Devtrack, Wikis, internal Web pages, QA Network/Proxy, Email, and Domain.
- Develop and maintain ongoing metrics for all Studio applications and services.
- Interface regularly with Studio customers to gather their needs and work with them on innovative solutions.
- Provide direction and teaching to junior sys admin(s) on the team.
- Participate in WW initiatives as directed by management.

Requirements
- BSc in Computer Science or equivalent computer experience.
- Experience with network device administration.

- Experience with Windows sys admin and web/wiki software.
- Excellent software troubleshooting abilities.
- Highly organized and communication and documentation skills.
- Independent worker as well as team player.

Recommended Certifications

C018, C012

J023 UNIX/Linux Administrator

Description

- Provide expert level Tier 3 technical infrastructure support services for issues elevated from the Support Center and other Technical Services groups.
- Diagnose and troubleshoot availability interruptions and other production issues. As well ensure reliable operation of production.
- Develop technical standards and evaluate IT vendor products.
- Maintain, monitor, and tune Production system and applications performance.
- Debug source code and performance problems and/or provides debugging assistance to developers.
- Identify opportunities to improve performance (eg, automating manual system tasks).
- Train and mentor staff. As well as resolve the most complex issues elevated from staff with less experience.
- Add, update, and close IT Problem Management database records.
- Research and resolve the most complex issues, and reviews related technology records to mitigate impact on assigned system.

Requirements

- Experience in Systems Administrator.
- Experience with Linux, UNIX and IBM WebSphere.
- Experience in UNIX/Linux Systems Administration.
- Experience with WebSphere Application Server.
- Experience with WAS in a multi-nodded, clustered environment.

Recommended Certifications

C017, C025, C043, C088

J024 UNIX Systems Administrator

Description

- Maintain and deploy applications in a high availability internet infrastructure and resolve hardware and software related problems.
- Install, configure, and upgrade servers, network hardware, and software applications and perform system backups and recovery.
- Performance system testing and planning. As well Support development team and development/testing environments.
- Provide 24x7 operations support.

Requirements

- Experience in systems administration and administrating (MySQL).
- Experience in administrating Linux and networking hardware.
- Experience in configuring and working with server hardware components (eg, RAID) and skills in scripting (PERL, shell).
- Strong organizational and verbal/written communication skills.

Recommended Certifications

C017, C018, C021

J025 Web Services Administrator

Description

- Support the development of the ISP/Web Services/Broadband websites with any programming functionality required.
- Provide second line support via the telephone to all ISP customers and escalate if necessary - using Gemini to log all calls and actions.
- Support customer websites by: providing any programming functionality required liaising with ISP to transfer domain names setting up sub-folders, email and client FTP areas via the remote dedicated server web page search engine optimization search engine registration testing of sites on Mac and Pc platforms, browsers and domain names registration and renewal generating monthly online web stat reports.
- Administration of the dedicated server.
- Assist in the production of web pages and undertake other assignments as requested by Senior Management.
- Online distribution of monthly e-marketing campaigns.

Requirements

- Experience in programming and web service administration.
- Excellent knowledge of HTML and Java script programming with knowledge of cascading style sheets and templates.
- Knowledge of CGI, Perl script, PHP, MySQL and server.

Requirements (Desired)

- Dreamweaver and Flash skills.

Recommended Certifications

C014, C021, C101, C103, C107, C150

J026 Website Administrator

Description

- Manage websites including design, websites content.
- Place new speakers on the website, photos, video clips, biographies, introductions and books and edit/update speaker data.
- Maintain hosting, network and web servers; maintain local copies of website as staging area for current work and as a backup.
- Create Video Clips from VHS or DVD media for the websites.

- Manage overall IT hardware/software/systems; including routine network administration; identifying need for IT improvement and making recommendations.

Requirements

- Experience in HTTP, FTP protocols and website design (HTML).
- Experience with MS Word, Dreamweaver, Photoshop, streaming video protocols, compression types and delivery mechanisms.
- Experience with Internet technology, Client/server environment, Windows and hosting services.
- Excellent problem solving skills and project management skills.
- Thorough understanding of database theory and application.
- Ability to independently research solutions for IT related problems and make solid recommendations to management.
- Ability to handle multiple-tasks and working independently.
- Scheduling and prioritizing tasks and projects.
- Maintaining an organized work area and effectively communication.

Requirements (Desired)

- Final Cut, MS Excel, Goldmine.

Recommended Certifications

C018, C103, C107, C110, C129

J027 Wintel Administrator

Description

- Daily support for windows system administration.
- Conversion of diverse server environments.

Requirements

- Experience in systems Administrator.
- Experience in Winsock/Wintel, NT Administration, IIS.
- Proficient in Windows Systems Administration.
- High availability configuration planning and management.
- Proficiency in IIS, either Veritas or Doubletake data replication configuration planning and management.

Recommended Certifications

C021

CHAPTER

6 COMPUTER DESIGNERS JOBS

Designer is a person that designs and prepares content for the World Wide Web, including text, images, site architecture and multimedia. Designing is the applied art of arranging image and text to communicate a message. It may be applied in any media, such as print, digital media, motion pictures, animation, product decoration, packaging, and signs. Web designers are sometimes just graphic artists, though most also write HTML.

J028 Designer using MyNetonomy product suite

Description

- Design solutions that meet the needs of the customer and the business, as well as help to deliver and implement them, throughout the project lifecycle.
- Work on applications developed using the MyNetonomy product suite, which is a web-based, front-end-customer, self-service component that interfaces through an enterprise application integration layer to legacy back end systems.
- Ensuring that quality and reliability standards are met at all times.

Requirements

- Experience in an IT application development or systems integration delivery role, ideally with business-critical.
- Experience of analyzing and breaking down problems and information using structured frameworks and methodologies.
- Experience in designing package-based solutions.

Requirements (Desired)

- Knowledge of the MyNetonomy product, Certified MyNetonomy Integrator.
- Understanding of J2EE technology, distributed systems, web application servers and middleware concepts.
- Managing the end-to-end delivery of solutions.

Recommended Certifications

C101, C150

J029 E-Learning Web Designer

Description

- Assist Art University faculties in developing web-based courses.
- Able to both assess and enhance the instructional value of content.

Requirements

- HTML, Dreamweaver, Flash, Adobe Acrobat, Fireworks and/or Photoshop, JavaScript, FTP and multimedia applications.
- Organizational ability and self-management and multi-tasking skills.
- Excellent oral/written communication.

Requirements (Desired)

- BA or equivalent experience required.
- Experience with action script, web-based training, XML, digital video production, audio editing, streaming media, and web conferencing.
- A fine arts and instructional background.

Recommended Certifications

C103, C105, C107

J030 Graphic Designer for Web and Mobile

Description
- Design and build games and other applications for Web.
- Design messaging interfaces, sports scores, dating services, etc. on the large screen (web) and the cell-phone handset screen.

Requirements
- CSS/HTML - including ability to do coding by hand.
- Understanding of user interface design.
- Good design eye, able to switch between genres.

Requirements (Desired)
- Macromedia Flash and 2D animation.
- Small screen pixel game art.
- Ability to install and configure your own machine.

Recommended Certifications
C103, C105, C107

J031 Information Architect

Description
- Analyze and reverse engineer transformation rules that are currently stored in SQL procedures and other systems.
- Catalog these rules for use in the TIBCO engine.
- Develop a new engine that transforms the files as received from the various sources and store and create an exception handling process for files that do not meet the necessary validations.
- Create and expedite testing process that allows intercept of files, translation, validation, and extraction in a more parallel process to allow for faster testing of file formats between SSB and other organizations.

Requirements
- Architect experience.
- Experience with SQL, TIBCO and SQL procedures.

Recommended Certifications
C129

J032 Interaction Designer

Description
- Prepare user interface specification documents consisting of wireframes, conceptual models, process flows, navigational maps, mock-ups, and/or interaction flow diagrams.
- Directly edit application source files, HTML and CSS.

- Contribute to, define, and enforce a user interface style guide that encompasses all externally-facing IronPort applications.
- Become an expert user of all IronPort products and services.
- Synthesize input from product management, engineering, quality assurance, customer support, systems engineers, customers, and other interaction designers to design and refine features.

Requirements

- Bachelor's degree.
- Strong visual design skills and experience rapidly prototyping visual designs for analyzing large data sets.
- Understanding of Internet and email standards, UNIX system administration, enterprise networking and security.
- Experience in a senior information design, user interface design, human factors engineering, or information architect position.
- Proven track record developing, delivering, and documenting high-quality user interface designs for technically complex web-based applications or UNIX system administration tools.
- Understanding of limitations in user interaction of command line interfaces, web-based applications, and thick-client applications and the ability to tailor designs for each medium.
- Excellent writing/oral communication and communication skills.

Recommended Certifications

C016, C018, C020

J033 Interactive UI design/web design

Description

- Work with Engineers, Art Directors, and Product Managers to design and implement Interactive Designs.
- Design user-interface (UI) elements based on existing styles, and create optimized graphics for Web site implementation.
- Create visual design solutions that address business, brand, market, and user requirements, including the design and production of screen layouts, color palettes, typography and UI elements.
- Provide creative solutions for a user-centric web experience.
- Propose and implement website redesign solutions.
- Participate in concept development and design ideation.
- Manage workflow and deadlines of multiple, simultaneous projects.

Requirements

- BSc in Graphic Design, Fine Arts, or related field.
- Interactive design experience.
- Solid portfolio with a range of creative samples that demonstrate relevant work or projects.
- Experience with user centered design and Icon design.
- Proficiency in screen layout and visual design.

- Proficiency with Macromedia Fireworks, or functional equivalents.
- Proficiency with HTML, DHTML, and CSS.
- Thorough knowledge of web design constraints.
- Solid understanding of web usability guidelines.
- Excellent strategic and conceptual skills.

Recommended Certifications

C107

J034 Mobile User Interface Designer

Description

- Work closely with Product Management and Engineering to define user models, streamline experiences, and produce both high-level flows and detailed mobile UI mockups.
- Design mobile interfaces that scale and extend elegantly.
- Think of creative solutions to complex problems, and proactively proposing improvements to the existing product.

Requirements

- Academic background in HCI, interaction design, or related field.
- Experience designing effective interfaces for mobile applications.
- Expert XHTML, WML, HTML, JavaScript, and CSS skills, as well as WAP knowledge and strong visual design sense.
- Ability to brainstorm well with other designers and give and take constructive feedback.

Requirements (Desired)

- Strong technical background.

Recommended Certifications

C107

J035 Scalability Architect

Description

- Work on challenging software engineering problems to scale online services that reach millions of people worldwide.
- Conceptualize unique technical approaches and drive your ideas through completion. As well as drive the design, development and implementation of crucial software and applications.
- Provide leadership in technology and software development processes, and mentor and coach other engineers.

Requirements

- Bachelor's degree in Computer Science or equivalent.
- Knowledge of various architectural, performance, and scalability issues. As well Java/J2EE, JSP, Servlets, JavaBeans, XML/SOAP.

- Significant experience developing distributed high performance computing solutions in Java/Linux.
- Commercial software development experience with high performance, scalable platforms. As well as experience in designing software to be robust, extensible and maintainable.
- Platform experience in Linux, Web servers and Application servers.
- Experience as a Team Lead and excellent verbal and written communications skills with the ability to influence others.

Requirements (Desired)

- Master's degree.

Recommended Certifications

C017, C056, C102, C109

J036 Senior Designer

Description

- Develop the graphic look, feel and user interface for sites.
- Understand and translate strategic goals and business requirements into visually compelling layouts.
- Concept, design and produce web site templates, page layouts etc.
- Communicate design concepts and strategies, verbally and visually.

Requirements

- Mastery of Adobe Photoshop and Adobe Illustrator.
- Experience designing online marketing and advertising including animated gif and flash ads, targeted landing pages, site promotions and page layouts.
- Experience with Web design, CSS and HTML/XHTML.
- Excellent web navigation, user-centered design and information design experience. As well as thorough knowledge of web usability issues, trends, and opportunities.
- Demonstrated strategic thinking, and creative problem solving abilities, to assist in meeting strategic goals.
- Strong interpersonal and communication skills, working in a team-based and working well in a highly collaborative environment.

Recommended Certifications

C105, C107

J037 Senior Developer/Architect

Description

- Provide best practice design and implementation techniques utilizing J2EE and web services.

Requirements

- BSc in Computer Science or related degree.
- Web/Internet related experience.

- Design and deploy large scale service oriented architecture.
- Hands-on web services experience in integration projects preferably with Portal front ends including BEA Portal and Plumtree.
- Hands-on development experience in Java, JSP, MVC/Struts, JDBC with particular focus on web services and related technologies including XML, XSL, UDDI, WSDL and Soap in robust high usage application scenarios on Weblogic or Web-Sphere.
- Provide SOA and web services best practices including techniques and best of breed tools for establishing web services management, security, performance, maintainability, development, and application integration.
- Excellent verbal and written communication skills.

Recommended Certifications

C029, C051, C056, C102

J038 Senior Interactive Designer

Description

- Create style-guides and design specs for specific projects.
- Brainstorm and conceptualize new projects as well as interpret design direction from creative director and implement on a project level.
- Take projects from inception to completion and manage designers and production staff on a project-by-project basis.
- Work with project managers to establish production timelines.
- Provide creative innovation for the projects you work on, and for the team as a whole. As well develop best practices, processes, and innovations to speed development timeline.
- Participate in client meetings and working in a team.

Requirements

- BA in graphic design, interactive design, animation, fine arts, advertising, or a related discipline.
- Professional digital design experience with a focus on illustration, character animation, and developing interactive media.
- Strong visual style and thorough understanding of how typography, layout, color, images and interactivity impact design.
- Knowledge of interactive Flash movies and proficiency with Action Script and create new assets entirely in Flash.
- Comfort with Photoshop, HTML, and vector graphics programs (Freehand/Illustrator), Swift 3D and Dreamweaver.
- Prior participation as a contributor to an interdisciplinary team (creative director, art director/senior interactive designer, other designers, project managers and instructional designers).
- Excellent communication, organizational, and verbal/written skills.

Requirements (Desired)

- Knowledge of capabilities and limitations of Web technologies such as HTML, JavaScript, AICC/SCORM, ColdFusion, AJAX, and CSS.

Recommended Certifications

C103, C104, C105, C106, C107

J039 Senior Software Architect

Description

- Design and implement the software architecture for a multi-tier ASP Application. As well create UML design artifacts from functional and detailed design requirements.
- Understand Oracle database and work with DBA.
- Perform unit, system and integration testing of all programming.
- Lead software design and architecture efforts.

Requirements

- BSc in Computer Science.
- Expert in all UML diagrams, J2EE, Java, XML and DB design.
- Experience as a lead software architect and have architected three software systems from inception through production.
- Recent experience with new technologies.
- Excellent communication skills and working in a team environment.

Recommended Certifications

C019, C056, C102, C138

J040 Senior Test Architect

Description

- Assist the QA/CCA Test Manager defining Acceptance Criteria, Service Level Agreements.
- Assist the QA/CCA Team in Go/No-Go decisions of project release/certifying releases for to Deployment/User Acceptance.
- Design IT Test strategy and setting direction for IT Testing.
- Manage the integration/testing of hardware and software solution components with an Application Development Test Plan.
- Develop appropriate plans, unit and system test scripts and procedures, test environment and data, and perform system level configuration and testing.
- Assume a team leadership role in the integration/validation of the solution components.

Requirements

- Certifications in the areas of software quality assurance or testing or quality assurance related certification(s).
- Test Engineer experience and Q/A Methodology.
- Hands-on experience leading information technology integration and testing of web application software components.
- Knowledge of all stages of Rapid Application Development of n-tier, Client/Server Solutions involving Enterprise Java technology using UML based iterative product

development methodologies such as Rational Unified Process (RUP) or Paradigm Plus.

- Experience in the use of UML based methodologies, in performance driven software development by use Case Oriented Rapid Application Development Cycles and multiple iterations of application assessment. As well experience with Object Oriented programming and scripting languages.

Recommended Certifications

C019, C102

J041 Senior User Interface Designer

Description

- Rapid prototyping from mock-ups through implementation including user flows, graphic design, coding, usability testing, and QA.
- Champion the user experience to upper management.
- Develop and run usability tests to validate your designs and iterating designs based on feedback.
- Create and customize UI options for key business partners and co-brands. As well as identify and lead process improvements to make UI design more efficient and effective.

Requirements

- BSc/MSc in Human Computer Interaction or equivalent work.
- Experience in front-end web design and development.
- Expert with Photoshop, Dreamweaver, XML/XLT, CSS, JavaScript, JSP, HTML. Java and Flash.
- Track-record of clean UI implementation.
- Able to work in a dynamic startup environment, self-motivated, detail-oriented and excellent communication skills.

Recommended Certifications

C056, C102, C103, C105

J042 Senior Web Designer

Description

- Design websites and manage external graphic development resource as well as online advertising creative (graphics and Flash).
- Provide informed, innovative recommendations regarding the use of Flash, ASP.NET, HTML, CSS, and DHTML.
- Take static files from design and reconstruct as needed to work with dynamic data. As well as create efficient, imaginative and sophisticated solutions to front-end problems.
- Function as liaison between design and development to ensure accurate implementation of specified design and functionality.
- Assess the technical feasibility of proposed designs.

- Evaluate workflow diagrams and initial mock-ups; make technology recommendations that support optimal construction, maintenance and performance. As well as estimate the time needed to complete the Integration phase of projects.
- Keep abreast of the latest developments in Internet technologies.

Requirements

- BA in Design, Web Design, Communications or equivalent.
- Proficiency in web design and all web development and design applications, Flash skills ad HTML hand-coding.
- Must be a skilled visual designer and web developer with experience/background in corporate web design and understanding of print campaign design-tie-ins.
- Superior UI and layout design skills.
- Ability to work well in a team and manage multiple client activities and project requests.
- Familiarity with PC environment and MAC OS.
- Experience with overseeing freelance editors and JavaScript.

Recommended Certifications

C103, C105, C107

J043 Senior Web/Print Designer

Description

- Design and maintain websites, direct mail, datasheets, online banners, email marketing.
- Work with the managers and senior graphic designer to develop clear marketing communications.

Requirements

- BSc Degree in Graphic Design or related studies.
- Professional experience in both web and print design.
- Experience with Photoshop, ImageReady, Illustrator, Dreamweaver and Flash. As well as programming skills.
- Strong typography, color and layout skills.
- Possess excellent organizational skills and high attention to detail.

Recommended Certifications

C103, C105

J044 User Interface Designer

Description

- Design and develop with a small team a Java-based WYSIWYG authoring tool to specify styling and data-binding for reports in a visual manner.
- Create and maintain user experience documents and detailed specs.

Requirements

- Must have extensive experience in Java Swing and design of WYSIWYG authoring tools.

- Knowledge of the strengths and weaknesses of Java UI frameworks, J2EE platform and web technologies.
- Intuitive understanding of good UI elements.

Recommended Certifications

C102

J045 Visual Designer

Description

- Develop websites visual layout and style.
- Collaborate with team members to make design decisions.
- Create web designs, graphics, and templates compatible with HTML/DHTML.

Requirements

- Bachelor or Master Degree in the visual arts and sciences.
- Professional web, software, and icon design experience.
- Expertise with web design, typography, color, and layout principles.
- Expertise with graphical software packages including Adobe Photoshop, Illustrator, and Macromedia Flash.
- Expertise with HTML/DHTML/CSS and familiarity with JavaScript.

Recommended Certifications

C103, C105, C107

J046 Web Designer

Description

- Design graphics, logos and animation for websites.
- Design new web interfaces, graphics and layouts.
- Image creation, optimization and manipulation.

Requirements

- Experience with Adobe PhotoShop and Macromedia Flash.
- Experience with Macromedia Dreamweaver and MS FrontPage.

Recommended Certifications

C103, C105

J047 Web Designer and Graphic Artist

Description

- Develop highly-structured small business websites; create templates from Photoshop files on a PC platform.
- Create and maintain e-commerce web sites on a PC platform.

Requirements

- Strong HTML, Dreamweaver and Adobe Photoshop skills.
- Competency with Adobe ImageReady.

- Flash with Action Scripting experience.
- Basic understanding of FrontPage.

Requirements (Desired)

- Experience with CSS.

Recommended Certifications

C103, C105, C106

J048 Web/Graphic Designer

Description

- Meeting with clients, project managers, and/or the design director to discuss the needs of a particular project.
- Interpret the project's needs, gathering information and data to clarify design issues, and thinking creatively to produce ideas and solutions to the design challenges, drawing from a strong background in usability and information design.
- Prepare multiple mock-ups and/or design options.
- Gathering feedback on design mock-ups and integrating necessary changes.
- Multi-tasking by working on multiple projects with concurrent deadlines, excellent time management.
- Using a wide range of media, including photography, illustration, or other mixed-media in design solutions.
- Produce accurate and high quality work.
- Make recommendations regarding production methods, materials needed, and costs.
- Keeping abreast of new design trends and design software developments.
- Working well in a team, with copywriters/editors, photographers, other designers, project managers, and clients and working to tight deadlines.

Requirements

- Bachelor of Arts degree in communication/graphic design or related field.
- Experience as a web/graphic designer.
- Facility with logo development.
- Experience with interface design for processes on the web, such as forms, shopping cart, and web-based functions.
- Solid sense of creativity, imagination, motivation, and the ability to "think outside of the box" to come up with innovative solutions to design challenges.
- Strong communication skills, with the ability to interpret clients' needs/ideas and the ability to clearly communicate design solutions to lay people.
- Strong knowledge of design software, especially Adobe Creative Suite (Photoshop, Illustration, Acrobat, and InDesign).
- An understanding of web usability, interface design, information architecture, visual marketing, and how people think and react to visual images.
- Strong attention to detail and the ability to accept criticism and successfully and creatively integrate design feedback.
- Working knowledge of printing and production methods.

- Ability to adhere to tight timelines and work well under pressure.

Requirements (Desired)

- Background or experience in color theory.

Recommended Certifications

C103, C105

J049 Web Multimedia Designer

Description

- Work closely with designers, programmers and marketing.
- Creating, producing, and optimizing graphics for various web interfaces as well as special projects based on platform requirements, in-house designs, and existing look and feel specifications.
- Working in a fast paced team environment, which often requires the ability to accommodate new priorities and special projects.
- Make recommendations on how to extend look and feel to new projects.
- Prepare content to these standards in JPG, GIF, HTML, and XML formats.

Requirements

- Strong sense of page layout and fundamentals of web-based graphic design.
- Web production experience in a work environment.
- High skill level in conceptual layout and color schemes with a strong understanding of web page layout, design, and graphics.
- Knowledge of Graphic Design, HTML, CSS, and basic JavaScript, Flash, Fireworks.
- Ability to take on a project and manage the work effectively, and complete it in a timely manner.
- High level of creativity.
- Ability to work independently in complex environments toward high-level goals.
- Strong communication, organization and presentation skills.
- Possess excellent interpersonal skills to work with different departments.
- Flexible to learn and utilize new web techniques and software.

Requirements (Desired)

- Degree in design/fine arts.

Recommended Certifications

C103, C105

J050 Web Portal Architect

Description

- Design, develop and support application solutions to meet client requirements.
- Design, develop and/or re-engineer highly complex application components.
- Integrate software packages, programs and reusable objects residing on multiple platforms.

Requirements

- Experience in digital design/Web development/design.
- Experience with large-scale information portals.
- Experience in developing major web presence for a B2B software solutions company, systems integrator or IT consultancy.
- Fluent in all aspects of website/digital production (Front and Back end).
- Online campaign experience, hands-on skills in Photoshop, Flash, HTML, Illustrator, Dreamweaver or ColdFusion, XML etc.

Recommended Certifications

C103, C105

CHAPTER

7 WEB DEVELOPERS JOBS

Web developer is a person or company that develops websites. A web developer handles all aspects of programming and scripting for a website. This includes adding pictures, client text, creating hyperlinks and implementing the site. A web developer can also act as web master and maintain/update the site once implemented. A web developer usually helps the client find a hosting company for their site.

J051 ASP.NET C# Web Developer

Description

- Develop a best-in-class managed website solution using leading edge architectures and technologies.
- The solution is centered on Content Management Server.
- Work as an independent contractor in a small team.

Requirements

- Experience with C# for ASP.NET and SQL Server programming and administration as well as XML, HTML, DHTML and JavaScript.
- Strong understanding of SourceSafe, IIS and Structured Software Development Methodologies (SDLS/MSF).
- Professional development experience as well as strong problem solving skills and ability to be proactive and make suggestions.
- Experiences working with design and development teams using a fast paced and structured develop process.
- Function well independently and with a team as well positive attitude, good communications skills and attention to detail.

Recommended Certifications

C056, C103, C107, C114, C116, C117, C118, C119, C120, C122, C125, C126, C127, C129

J052 Aviation Application Developer

Description

- Develop analysis and system software for aviation weather applications.
- Participate in a team environment to support multiple aspects of the project, including Infrastructure written in C++.
- Utilize custom in-house software and commercial products.

Requirements

- Bachelor's degree in Computer Science, Electrical Engineering, Physics, Applied Math, System Engineering, or equivalent with programming experience.
- Experience with Java, C++, C, and computer operating systems including LINUX, and Solaris.
- Understanding of software engineering methodology and experience with both object-oriented analysis and design.
- Able to work in a team and good oral/written communication skills.

Requirements (Desired)

- Real-Time software development experience using JAVA and C++ under the Linux operating system.
- Experience with middleware, web services, and the mapping of geographic information on a display.

Recommended Certifications

C017, C100, C101, C102, C150

J053 C/C++ Senior Developer

Description

- Develop security applications and enhance other applications.
- Work on development team dealing with middle office and back office applications.

Requirements

- Developer experience.
- Experience with UNIX, Sybase, Java, C++, C and Corba.

Requirements (Desired)

- Any experience Rogue Wave tools.

Recommended Certifications

C020, C100, C101, C102, C150

J054 C/C++/Oracle Senior Developer

Description

- Reverse engineering of the business logic/transformation rules in the Oracle stored procedures.
- Move the business logic/transformation rules to TIBCO.
- Transfer data (flat files) using a utility like FTP.

Requirements

- Developer experience.
- Experience with PL/SQL, Oracle, Pro*C, Java, C++ and C.
- Experience with TIBCO (Tibco Message Broker).

Recommended Certifications

C047, C100, C101, C102, C138, C141

J055 ColdFusion and MS SQL Server Master

Description

- Build and maintain new database functionalities using ColdFusion and MS SQL Server. As well as build and maintain new reports using ColdFusion and Crystal Reports.
- Design and implement additions and modifications to the company's relational database and maintain security of Database.
- Index existing database tables for improved performance.
- Build end user forms with ColdFusion and JavaScript form validation and document new and existing code.
- Maintain the organization's email serve and inner-office LAN.

- Maintain all technical aspects of inner-office environment.

Requirements
- BSc in Computer Science.
- Experience with ColdFusion and MS SQL Server.
- Knowledge of reporting software such as Crystal Reports.
- Creative team player and great verbal and communication skills.

Recommended Certifications
C001, C104, C129

J056 ColdFusion Developer

Description
- Develop and produce a new search engine.
- Other web based development duties as required.

Requirements
- Experience in web-application-development with solid coding skills and web design.
- Knowledge of ColdFusion and database development.
- Ability to work as part of a small team.

Recommended Certifications
C104, C107

J057 Custom Software Developer

Description
- Build and modify custom business applications (Web Applications, Database Applications, eCommerce and Application Integration).
- Responsible of systems analysis, design, coding, testing, debugging, installation, support and other technical tasks work.
- Write documentation to describe programming development, logic, and coding.

Requirements
- BSc in Computer Science or equivalent.
- Development experience with Microsoft .NET Technologies.
- Knowledge of XML, XSL, HTML, ASP, ASP.NET, C#, and/or VB.NET, Microsoft SQL Server & TSQL and/or Oracle & PL/SQL.
- Strong understanding of the custom development SDLC.
- Strong written and verbal communication skills.

Requirements (Desired)
- Experience in the consulting industry.
- Knowledge of Insurance brokers, agencies, carriers.

Recommended Certifications

C014, C056, C103, C107, C114, C116, C117, C118, C119, C120, C122, C125, C126, C127, C129, C138

J058 Database Application Developer

Description
- Develop applications on MS SQL-Server and SQL programming.
- Develop applications on VBA/MS-Access.

Requirements
- Experience with Visual Basic and ASP programming.
- Experience with MS Access development, VBA.
- Experience with MS SQL-Server and SQL programming.
- Ability to develop and support new and existing applications.
- Detail oriented and analytical problem solving skills.

Requirements (Desired)
- Exposure to .NET framework.
- Familiarity with Investment Management business.

Recommended Certifications

C014, C112, C114

J059 Desktop Software Developer

Description
- Work with QA analysts to resolve issues before going live.
- Work with project managers to implement features that enhance the overall user experience.
- Interface with graphic designers to assist with front-end development.

Requirements
- Experience with C#.
- Proficient in Instant Message Development.
- Working knowledge of Socket Server communications.
- Ability to create software installation tools and product updaters.
- Self-motivated problem solver, excellent written and oral communication skills.

Recommended Certifications

C108, C111, C114

J060 Developer - .NET C#, SQL Server, IIS

Description
- Work with IT Technical Director to maintain and develop current database with a Back End of SQL Server and Front End of C#.

- Work with marketing department to assist in architecture, design, development, implementation and maintenance of the intranet.
- Maintain the website, content management of the site will also be expected and provide enhancements and development on systems.
- Effective communication and good project management of tasks.

Requirements

- Experience in web development and design in a commercial environment.
- Proficient in C# programming and solid knowledge of SQL server.
- Good web skills (IIS), web design tools (Adobe suite, Macromedia).

Requirements (Desired)

- Web technology knowledge (HTML, XHTML, ASP, XML, and JavaScript) and Knowledge of photo-editing packages.
- Proactive approach to problem solving, ability to follow these through to conclusion.
- Self-motivated, desire to deliver excellent customer service.
- Organization and communication skills and ability to prioritize workload; work under pressure and to deadlines on own initiative.

Recommended Certifications

C103, C105, C106, C107, C108, C114, C119, C126, C129

J061 Dynamic HTML Coder

Description

- Create HTML directly by hand not utilizing a generator for enterprise level web pages.

Requirements

- Web developer experience and HTML.

Recommended Certifications

C103, C107

J062 Flash Game Developer

Description

Create top quality flash based online games and integrating them.

Requirements

- Game development experience.
- Experience with online game programming using Flash (Action script) and/or Director (Lingo) and experience with multi-user game.
- Creativity in game designs advanced level in animation skills.
- Ability to work well with others and with minimal supervision.

Recommended Certifications

C105, C106

J063 Interdev Web Developer

Description
- Implementation of the LCIP rewrite enhancement. The LCIP rewrite will be a web-enabled application with an Oracle RDBMS.
- The web GUI will kick off many Oracle stored procedures to do most of the data processing.
- Lead team members in development and technical matters and assist to trouble shoot issues.

Requirements
- Web developer experience.
- Experience with ASP, JavaScript, Oracle.
- Experience with Microsoft Visual Interdev and DHTML.

Recommended Certifications
C103, C107, C108, C119, C138, C141

J064 Internet Database Developer

Description
- Create/support database designs and systems.
- Assist project managers, clients and other developers to create high-performance.
- Reliable/secure databases and develop dynamic, database-driven websites as well configure/administer database servers.
- Import, export, manipulate data & automate functions.

Requirements
- Database developer experience.
- Experience with Java, ASP, Perl, SQL server and Linux.
- Experience with HTML, CGI Scripting, PHP.

Recommended Certifications
C017, C100, C102, C103, C114, C129

J065 Junior VB.NET Developer

Description
- Work in a fast-paced environment as part of a team of .NET Developers.
- Enhance internal web-based processing applications.
- Maintenance work on VB/SQL applications and new development work using .NET.

Requirements
- Bachelor's degree in Computer Science or related field; or equivalent education/professional experience.
- Educational experience with Visual Basic, SQL Server, and Classic ASP Development.

- Solid work experience with VB Scripting, VB.NET, ASP.NET.
- Solid verbal and written communication skills.
- Solid work ethic, willingness to work hard and learn very quickly.

Recommended Certifications
C125, C126, C127, C129

J066 Java ColdFusion Developer

Description
- Registration/confirmation ColdFusion (BUD) database for Joint Programs and a Metrics Suite of online tools (easier database/reporting).
- Capable for Corporate e-Business to produce customized departmental and corporate level metrics reporting.

Requirements
- Application Developer experience.
- Experience with Java, ColdFusion, DHTML, XML and SQL Server.
- Experience with XHTML, CSS, JavaScript, SQL/t-SQL (stored procedures, triggers, etc - on SQL Server).

Requirements (Desired)
- Fusebox Framework.

Recommended Certifications
C014, C056, C102, C103, C104, C129, C150

J067 Lead Server Developer

Description
- Backend server development of an online consumer service.
- Design, develop and implement components of a robust and scaleable web system.
- Planning of software releases to deliver functionality.
- Modeling and implementation of required performance and reliability for the production site.

Requirements
- BSc and/or MSc in Computer Science.
- Experience in backend server development, database-based software design, transaction management software.
- Software development experience at a top-notch software company, with proven track record in shipping products from conception to delivery and next generation software.
- Ability in programming for the web – JSP, JAVA, J2EE, Servlets, beans, XML, JavaScript, server-side information retrieval, Oracle PL/SQL, etc.
- Ability to conceptualize and rapidly prototype from marketing and business requirements.

- Multi-browser support, knowledge of file formats and files transfer across platforms.

Requirements (Desired)

- Prior startup experience.

Recommended Certifications

C014, C100, C101, C102, C114, C138, C141, C150

J068 Mobile Wireless Application Developer

Description

- Build embedded, native and J2ME applications on a range of handsets, making the web and web services available on mobile platforms.
- Making the world's information universally accessible and useful - at any time and in any place.

Requirements

- BSc/MSc/PhD in Computer Science or equivalent.
- Extensive experience programming in C/C++ and Java.
- Experience in J2ME/Symbian/BREW/Windows Mobile/Palm OS and other mobile environments/languages.

Requirements (Desired)

- Development experience with handsets.

Recommended Certifications

C100, C101, C102, C150

J069 Oracle Database Developer

Description

- Implementation of data transformation processes.
- Supporting application development.
- Supporting of Business Analysts with adhoc queries.
- Troubleshooting performance bottlenecks and data anomaly issues

Requirements

- Experience with Oracle Import/Export, SQL Tuning, Schema Objects Management and Table Reorganization.
- Hands-on PL/SQL (stored procedures, packages, triggers).
- Good UNIX shell scripting.

Requirements (Desired)

- VLDB/Data Warehousing, Replication and Perl scripting.
- Java programming, Linux and SQL Server.

Recommended Certifications

C017, C100, C102, C114, C129, C138, C139, C140, C141

J070 PHP Web Developer

Description
- Improve/integrate systems already developed in-house.
- Extend existing open-source applications, and implement new internal and client facing applications.
- Work with already existing code, work with clients to develop/polish requirements and work with ad-hoc teams.

Requirements
- Bsc/BA in Computer Science or associated field.
- Experience in developing PHP applications.
- Experience in developing web application using MySQL.
- Advanced knowledge of HTML, JavaScript, CSS and AJAX.
- Strong experience with XML and associated technologies.
- Good understanding of how APIs work, how to integrate them and the ability to quickly learn new APIs.
- Strong written and oral communication skills.

Requirements (Desired)
- Experience using LDAP, Smarty, Swishe, Mac Platform, SVN and Oracle.

Recommended Certifications
C056, C103, C107, C138

J071 Senior Developer for Speech Applications

Description
- Install Nuance software in client environments.
- Develop/test code for client (and sometimes internal) projects.
- Integrate and debug complex software, often with untested stacks.
- Debug complex issues stemming from unknown sources.
- Coordinate with clients as necessary, with guidance from project managers and work with Speech UI designers.
- Create a system design documents.
- Help mentor and guide junior developer resources.

Requirements
- BSc in Computer Science.
- Understand Nuance products for implementation.
- Experience working with backend, middleware, various databases.
- Java/web architecture experience.
- Technical mindset with ability to see the bigger picture.
- Quick to ramp up to new technologies, ability to work well on multiple efforts simultaneously and strong communication skills.

Requirements (Desired)
- Pro Svcs background.

- Voice or UI background (as is music/audio engineering).

Recommended Certifications

C102, C103, C107, C129, C138

J072 Senior Java Developer

Description

- Analyze, design, write program code, test, document, and implement functionally appropriate, technically sound, and well-integrated application systems.
- Respond to production problems and implement immediate resolution efforts across technology areas.
- Provide Leadership as a communications liaison between the business customer and the technology development and support groups and provide Leadership for system and acceptance testing.
- Develop detail program specifications, evaluate and recommend emerging technologies and influence technical designs.
- Develop time esteems for project schedules, monitor progress and provide accurate and timely reports.
- Advanced mentoring and coaching others to prevent problems from reoccurring. As well as develop cost and benefit analysis.
- Plan and manage projects activities within allocated resources.
- Negotiate and manage team relationships at project level.
- Analyze and resolve complex or multiple problems. Also research and recommend alternative actions for problem resolution.
- Employ productivity aids in all aspects of assignments.
- Facilitate or complete Analysis, design, and programming of viable solutions to high complexity business problems according to user specifications.
- Identify process or system enhancements for business Customers.

Requirements

- Software Engineer experience.
- Programmer Analyst experience.
- Experience with Java, HTML, EJB, JSP, IBM WebSphere, XML, UNIX Scripting. OOD, OOM, J2EE and STRUTs.
- Experience with SDLC, OO analysis and design and UML.
- Working with relational databases, preferably Oracle.
- Experience with JMS, Swing, Clearcase, GUI Design, MQ Series, WebSphere, WSAD IDE, and Synergy.
- Writing and debugging stored procedures and working with a Persistence Framework, Context Support, LDAP, Code review and static analysis.
- Writing UNIX shell scripts, writing ANT scripts, and Project Management skills.
- IT experience on multiple platforms/technologies.
- Strong experience with problem-solving abilities.
- Strong verbal communication skills and strong Leadership skills.

Recommended Certifications

C014, C019, C027, C028, C029, C053, C055, C056, C100, C102, C103, C114, C129, C138, C139

J073 Senior Symbian/Mobile Developer

Description

- Design, develop and test high-performance embedded applications for mobile devices in both Java and C++.
- Co-design and implement best of breed end-to-end architectures for future software products.
- Conduct R&D activities surrounding developing mobile telecom standards and new software platforms for mobile devices (eg, mobile Linux).
- Facilitate good software development practices with close regard for continuous improvement of company's software development methodology.
- Traveling to support onsite product deployment.

Requirements

- Experience in designing and developing C++ for mobile devices, PDAs or embedded platforms and embedded real time systems.
- Experience with device platforms such as Palm OS, J2ME, Symbian and BREW platforms.
- Experience in developing voice, PTT (Push to Talk), SMS, MMS or other applications.
- Thorough knowledge of mobile networking concepts and internet protocols: SIP, VoIP, GSM, CDMA, and WCDMA standards.
- Keen understanding of the tradeoffs required when choosing java vs. native applications on resource constrained devices.
- Expertise of object-oriented design and implementation and turn ideas and concepts into carefully designed and well-authored code.
- Solid understanding of performance analysis and software optimization in embedded, real time software environments.
- Experience with the complete software lifecycle. As well as strong end-to-end understanding of wireless data and voice services.
- Superior embedded/Real Time software debugging skills.
- Experience leading small teams and mentoring junior developers.

Requirements (Desired)

- Experience with POOM, Pocket Outlook, Java, Apache/Tomcat, Linux/Solaris, WebSphere, HTML/XML, JSP, IMAP, Servlets, Struts, WAP, SyncML, iMode, proxy servers, HTTP, TCP/IP.
- Knowledge and experience with unified messaging technologies, SIP servers, media servers and announcement/IVR servers.
- Experience with telecom service creation environments (SCE), telecom provisioning, billing and operational systems (BSS/OSS).

Recommended Certifications

C004, C017, C019, C027, C028, C029, C055, C056, C100, C101, C102, C103, C150

J074 Sharepoint Developer

Description

- Develop, integrate and implement multiple Sharepoint sites for several lines of businesses.
- Create training guides and teach users how to maintain and develop their Sharepoint sites.
- Gather requirements from the user on the Sharepoint site.
- Create the front-end user interface and format for the sites.

Requirements

- Experience in Sharepoint development and implementation.
- Experience leading project implementations and training users with new software technology.
- Highly motivated, goal oriented and excellent communication skills.
- Ability to work well in a team environment, as well as teach others.
- Excellent verbal and written communication skills.

Recommended Certifications

C019

J075 Software/Hardware Design Developer

Description

- A part of a team tasked with delivering a revolutionary data collection and analysis system.
- The work carries a high level of importance, and offers direct participation in unique problem solving, testing approaches, and extensive research.

Requirements

- Bachelor's degree in Computer Science, Computer/Electrical Engineering, or Mathematics.
- Experience with Data Indexing/Information Retrieval.
- Experience with Distributed Systems/Network Programming.
- Experience with Real Time Embedded System Development Command and Control, and Software Development/Object Oriented Programming.
- Experience with J2EE Development/BEA Weblogic Application Server and Hardware Descriptive Languages (VHDL, Verilog).

Recommended Certifications

C004, C018

J076 SQL Developers

Description

- Develop a new TIBCO engine that transform the files as received from the various sources and store.

- Create an exception handling process for files that do not meet the necessary validations.
- Create and expedite testing process that allows intercept of files, translation, validation, and extraction in a more parallel process to allow for faster testing of file formats between SSB and other organizations

Requirements
- Developer experience.
- Strong Development of SQL, SQL procedures and TIBCO.

Recommended Certifications
C114, C129

J077 Talented Perl Developer

Description
- Help build web applications for websites.
- Create code-base very clean and well-commented, but not object-oriented, on FreeBSD, running Apache/mod_perl and MySQL.

Requirements
- Experience with Perl (mod_perl) and SQL (MySQL).
- Experience with HTML and JavaScript.

Recommended Certifications
C103, C114

J078 VBA Developer

Description
- Develop applications to feed data into financial reporting system.
- Work closely with manager to ensure approach/development progress is consistent with project goals.
- Import and reformat data from multiple sources into a 3rd party Financial Reporting system.

Requirements
- Developer experience.
- Experience with Visual Basic, SQL Server and SQL development.
- VBA development experience (eg, Microsoft Access).
- Expertise in data capture and reformatting to system specs.
- Experience in unit testing development.
- Knowledge in Fund Accounting and Fund Administration.
- Strong analysis and documentation skills.
- Excellent verbal and written communication skills.

Recommended Certifications
C114, C129

J079 VB .NET Web Developer

Description
- Modify existing applications to connect to a product called Verastream to offer product updates for the internal users.

Requirements
- Experience three tiered web development.
- Experience developing in VB.NET, XML and SQL.
- Fluent in T-SQL, Stored procedures and very comfortable writing databases, tables and triggers.
- Experience with web services and converting web applications from VB 6.0 to VB .NET.

Requirements (Desired)
- BizTalk.

Recommended Certifications
C056, C114, C122, C125, C126, C127, C128, C129

J080 VB/Mainframe Web Developer

Description
- Work with some of the newest technology being employed by the organization and be challenged by a variety of programming assignments that deal with the creation, management and delivery of HTML content.
- The projects in this division make use of such technologies as Message Brokering, VB, Web and Mainframe programming.

Requirements
- Web developer and Programmer experience.
- Experience with HTML, Visual Basic, COM, CICS, DB2, COBOL and ASP.

Recommended Certifications
C026, C104, C107, C119

J081 Vignette Developer

Description
- Redesign the corporate website including: Change the graphic look of the site, minimize page load times by reducing use of graphics.
- Create new database templates for serving up content via Vignette.

Requirements
- Experience with HTML and web developer experience.
- Vignette experience.

Recommended Certifications
C103, C119

J082 Web Application Developer

Description
- Assist in the implementation of the CRM/e-commerce platform, including integration with other related systems.
- Responsible for ongoing maintenance and development of CRM system, and carry out other technical and site administration duties.
- Work with the E-Commerce team to identify and define additional functionality as well work with the applications team.

Requirements
- BSc degree or equivalent experience.
- Experience with application development, database development or web development and recent ASP and/or Visual Basic.
- Solid understanding of business applications, web/internet applications and database technologies.
- Experience/expertise with Microsoft Windows environment and infrastructure, including Microsoft Windows Server, Microsoft IIS, Microsoft SQL Server, XML, .NET, HTML and CSS.
- Ability to translate business processes into technical solutions.
- Experience with one major ERP/CRM enterprise application.
- Strong demonstrated teamwork skills.
- Good leadership, planning and organization skills.

Requirements (Desired)
- Onyx Enterprise CRM.
- Experience with source control management, web services and content syndication.

Recommended Certifications
C014, C056, C103, C107, C108, C112, C117, C118, C119, C122, C125, C126, C127, C129, C138, C141

J083 Web-Based Application Developer

Description
- A full-time expert in web-based, client-side technologies is needed for research and development of a portal to a large, distribute, interconnect, virtual database of visual media.
- Work as research collaborator generating ideas and Work in a multidisciplinary research environment.
- Analytical skills will be extremely useful for experimentation on the utility of tools and evaluations of system performance.
- Teach and mentor colleagues who are experts in other fields, but who may have little experience in web-based applications.

Requirements
- PhD, MSc or BSc degree (or equivalent work experience) in Information Technology or related computer discipline.

- Experience with Java, J2EE, Eclipse, JavaScript, Ajax, XML, Swing, and Spring.
- Experience with Flash Media, Action Script, and related tools.
- Strong communication and interpersonal skills with an eagerness to learn, invent, and share.

Requirements (Desired)

- Experience in disciplined software engineering.

Recommended Certifications

C056, C100, C101, C102, C105, C106, C107, C119, C150

J084 WebMethods Developer

Description

- Develop WebMethods flow services.
- Understand and follow requirements documents, design and coding standards, perform unit and component level testing.
- Follow all change management and control standards.

Requirements

- Application developer experience.
- Java, XML, WebMethods, PL/SQL, Oracle.
- Experience in Integrations across Enterprise EAI and B2B using WebMethods.
- Experience in Integration Server, Broker, Trading Networks, Oracle Applications Adapter, JDBC Adapter, XML, Java, and SQL knowledge.

Requirements (Desired)

- EDI, Rational ClearCase.
- UNIX knowledge.

Recommended Certifications

C056, C100, C102, C108, C118, C138, C141, C150

J085 WebSphere Developer

Description

- Use WebSphere WCS development tools in a MQ-Series environment to integrate a legacy AS/400 CRM application.
- Write business process functionality using WAS or WCS.

Requirements

- Web Developer experience.
- Experience with JSP and IBM WebSphere.
- WCS development tools and commands experience.

Requirements (Desired)

- Aspect Tools, Kana E-Mail, MQ-Series.

Recommended Certifications

C029, C014, C053, C100, C102, C119, C122

J086 Windows Systems Developer

Description
- XO Communications hosts many complex websites.
- Assist in further developing hosting platform.
- Work on any and all levels of the product, including handling problem escalations against current live systems.
- Develop new features and work with the rest of team.

Requirements
- Deep into internals and integration of Microsoft technologies like MS-SQL Server, Windows Server, IIS, ASP/ASP.NET and others.

Recommended Certifications
C103, C107, C108, C114, C117, C118, C119, C120, C122, C125, C126, C127, C129

CHAPTER

8 COMPUTER ENGINEERS JOBS

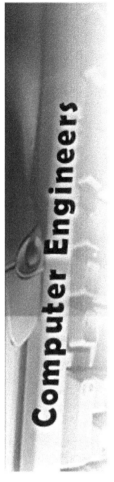

Engineer is a person who is responsible for designing and programming large-scale computer systems and applications. Similar to a systems analyst, software engineers primarily design and build complex system software, such as operating systems, protocol architectures, or databases upon which application software programs will run. Software engineering is the profession concerned with creating and maintaining software applications by applying technologies and practices from computer science, project management, engineering, application domains, and other fields.

J087 Analyst, Quality Standards

Description
- Develop measures to gauge accuracy and quality of products.
- Perform analysis to measure and validate the accuracy of the products versus the internal benchmarks.
- Perform analysis to measure the performance of the products versus the Service Level Agreements for accuracy established with clients.
- Analyze and interpret product quality issues through careful reconciliation of data against other sources.
- Support account management through detailed analytical projects in response to client-raised concerns about accuracy.
- Prepare reports on product quality for the executive team and various product teams.

Requirements
- Bachelor's degree and outstanding academic credentials.
- Professional experience in a quantitative analysis role.
- Strong problem solving ability and analytical insight.
- Expert-level skills in Microsoft Excel.
- Extensive experience accessing and analyzing large sets of data through SQL queries and working knowledge of Database Structures and Database Design Theory.
- Ability to present and communicate concepts, ideas, analyses, and conclusions to both technical and business audiences.
- Background in statistics and experience with SAS.
- Experience working in a cross-functional environment with several interacting teams and ability to work on multiple projects in parallel while managing constantly changing deadlines and priorities.
- Experience in the field of market research or marketing intelligence.
- Strong organizational and oral/written communication skills.

Recommended Certifications
C109, C112, C114, C129

J088 Content Development Engineer

Description
- Understand company product and business strategies and propose and develop web content and initiatives to meet these strategies.
- Manage user studies and other customer research, use web analysis tools to drive web strategies.
- Create new web content and revise existing content to see that it supports customer needs and company-wide strategies.
- Take a lead role in site navigation, features, and structure, so users can quickly find product and applications information.
- Determine the structure and taxonomy used to present product lines and makes creative use of company state-of-the-art parametric and web database systems.

Requirements
- Web Master experience.
- Experience with Java, HTML, Web design and user interface.
- Web marketing experience including formulation of pages, web user research, user interface, and analytics.
- Broad electrical engineering knowledge with experience in analog/mixed-signal design or applications.
- Ability to understand technical information, products, applications, and end-markets quickly.

Recommended Certifications
C014, C019, C100, C102, C103, C107, C109, C112, C119

J089 CRM Integration

Description
- Oversee and implement custom deployments of product suite for clients as well as estimate and manage implementation projects.
- Integrate applications with Oracle, PeopleSoft, SAP, and other backend enterprise systems using ETL, XML, and/or other scripting languages.
- Work with customer IT organizations and development team.

Requirements
- Experience in Systems Integrator, Software Engineer and Call Center Manager.
- Experience with Siebel, CRM, HTML, JavaScript, XML, PHP, Perl, Oracle, UNIX, Linux, UNIX Administration, SUN/Solaris, ETL, Python, MySQL, PostgreSQL and SQL Server.

Requirements (Desired)
- Familiarity with enterprise applications in call centers (eg, Avaya,Siebel, Genesys).

Recommended Certifications
C017, C019, C056, C103, C113, C114, C129, C138, C139, C140, C141, C149

J090 Deployment Engineer

Description
- Develop and evolve a deployment automation framework.
- Take a project from concept to launch as the primary technical contact. As well work with multiple clients concurrently, each with different architectures and requirements.
- Provide deployment, release, and environmental management for all web software applications on a consistent basis.
- Design and implement of a change management system for updating and synchronizing software in a grid environment.

Requirements
- BSc in Computer Science or Engineering.
- Experience in deployment for an ISP, ASP or grid provider.

- Successful deployment of complex web-application in scalable, HA scenario, JBOSS Application, PostgreSQL Database, FibreChannel and RAID technologies.
- Significant direct experience implementing, troubleshooting, and supporting Linux/UNIX, Internet based applications, Apache web servers, Java application servers and Apache load-balancing.
- Deep knowledge of JBOSS clustering and PostgreSQL (development and tuning DBA level).
- Comfortable in open source deployment. Also implemented a change management system in a web hosting or grid environment.
- Experience with installations of components for use in a web environment and migrations from development environments through production required.
- Solid understanding of web technologies, internet protocols, J2EE, PHP, JSP, SQL, PKI, RedHat and SuSE Linux administration.
- Excellent customer skills and able to work in very stressful customer situations. In addition, small/large projects management experience in the internet business arena.
- Use of "blade" technology, not monolithic servers.
- Strong organizational and communication skills.

Recommended Certifications
C003, C004, C014, C017, C019, C100, C109, C112, C114, C122, C129, C147, C148

J091 EBAY Software Engineer

Description
- Design, implement, and test new features for eBay Data Management tools. As well share release management duties on feature rollouts, share on-call responsibilities.
- Provide engineering support to business and QA organizations, including bug triage and product/system administration.
- Segment and design system layers to support componentized and layered application development, including user interface, business functionality, and database access.
- Work with other engineers, managers, Product Management, QA, and Operations teams to develop innovative solutions that meet market needs with respect to functionality, performance, reliability, realistic implementation schedules, and adherence to development goals and principles.
- Define, design, and implement software applications. In addition estimate engineering effort and plan implementation.
- Independently design code and test major features, as well as work jointly with other team members to deliver complex changes.

Requirements
- BSc in Computer Science or related field.
- Develop industry and product technical expertise.
- Strong design/development experience on Java, C++, UNIX, Java, Swing, DB, HTML, ISAPI, CGI, Perl, shell and RDBMS (Oracle).
- Experience in requirements analysis, design, coding and unit testing of scalable, distributed, fault-tolerant applications in NT and UNIX environments.

Requirements (Desired)
- MSc in Computer Science.

Recommended Certifications
C014, C100, C102, C109, C114, C122, C129, C138, C140, C141

J092 Escalation Engineer

Description
- Resolve and document customer support issues as escalated by operations and provide world-class service to customers.
- Track historical support issues and customer complaints/requests.
- Work with engineering to document existing problems/bugs. As well as provide technical leadership throughout Engineering.
- Provide feedback into software engineering and product management roadmap relative to known problems, inefficiencies, and customer feature requests of existing products.
- Provide continual and ongoing training of operations personnel to reduce escalations and foster more independence.
- Work closely with operations to develop ongoing processes for handoff, accounting and documentation of each support escalation.
- Develop tools to automate lab, engineering, and support processes.
- Establish, maintain, and enforce the company's network standards.
- Represent engineering at meetings with customers.

Requirements
- Experience with UNIX-based, RedHat Linux, Debian Linux, FreeBSD, SunOS and TCP/IP networking protocols.
- Experience with IP and its test/troubleshooting features as it applies to inter-network routing and TCP/IP network management tools.
- Knowledge of RIP, OSPF, BGP in a large-scale inter-networking environment, C, Perl and UNIX Shell programming, and TCP/IP network management and network engineering applications.
- Working knowledge of UNIX systems utilities (eg, BASH, SH, Perl, AWK, SED, RCS, CVS, etc).
- Implementing routing policies through access lists, filters, and AS-Path controls.
- Experience and success performing customer service in the support of complex applications and/or systems.

Recommended Certifications
C003, C004, C005, C006, C007, C016, C017, C018, C109, C145, C146, C147, C149

J093 Flash Software Engineer

Description
- Design and develop Action Script-based media clients.

Requirements
- Experience designing and implementing parsing/filtering software.

- Experience commercial software development with Flash, Shockwave and Macromedia Action Script.
- Experience with C++, .NET, MS Visual Studio, HTML, JavaScript, CSS, XML, SOAP, and protocol development.
- Experience with Flash file management shared object software, use of Action Script for client/server communication.
- Highly motivated self starter and team player.
- Strong communication and documentation skills.

Recommended Certifications
C056, C103, C105, C106, C107, C122

J094 Internet Technical Analyst

Description
- Assist in management of web technical environment, coordination and monitoring efforts of third-party contractor currently managing environment.
- Manage and track Web software and hardware support and licenses, domain name registration.
- Assist in management of web site technical development projects; may include design of scope and functionality of application, delivery of specifications to developer, as well as testing.
- Assist in troubleshooting and maintenance of web commerce environment, most generally relating to product administration and database.
- Assist in providing technical direction for Web technical environment.
- Act as technical liaison between web and in-house teams.
- Participate in other Web-Related projects as supervisor directs.
- Interface with IS, Internet, Merchandising, Creative personnel and management at various levels.
- Interface with out-source MSP's and development personnel.

Requirements
- Experience with, SQL Plus, PL/SQL, Oracle database, UNIX/Sun servers, and Cisco networking equipment systems administration.
- Knowledge of Sun servers/OS, Oracle DB, ATG commerce engine.
- Experience with Adobe Photoshop, Illustrator routers and firewalls.
- Strong organizational, project management and troubleshooting skills. As well ability to communicate effectively with users and with technical people.
- Ability to work in a collaborative environment and able to deliver results under tight deadlines and in a wide variety of disciplines.

Recommended Certifications
C019, C114, C138, C140, C141, C149

J095 IQA engineer

Description
- Provide quality assurance for international features and test internationalized and localized software for client product.
- Test compatibility with major websites in international markets, the creation and maintenance of test suites, execution of test suites, problem research and reporting.
- Follow project milestones, design, implement, document, and/or execute test, evaluate and communicate results, and investigate product features (including ad hoc testing).

Requirements
- Test engineer experience and QA engineer experience.
- Experience with QA Methodology, HTML, JavaScript, Linux, SML and CSS.

Recommended Certifications
C017, C103

J096 IT Support Engineer

Description
- Provide 1st level support for all desktop hardware, TWP applications, and audio-visual issues for all TWP users which include the Trading Floor, PCD, Investment Banking, Finance, Research, HR, Property Management, and/or TWP clients.
- Monitor and respond to client emails (Technical Support mailbox) and Help Desk calls.
- Monitor and track trouble calls via the Team Track ticketing system.
- Participate in the daily on-call support engineer rotation.
- Assist with client conferences as requested including computer and phone conferencing setup, onsite support.
- Setup and coordinate audio visual meetings in conference rooms.
- Diagnose problems and troubleshoot all TWP standard equipment, Desktops, laptops and printers.
- Address user Move/Change: Relocate and setup user equipment (computer and phones).
- Address equipment, training and support issues upon the arrival of new hires and on employee exit.
- Create and deploy Desktop/Laptop images utilizing the Symantec Ghost Solution Suite and Client Migration utilities.
- Test and apply all OS and Application patches, fixes and upgrades on TWP desktops and laptops.
- Perform Microsoft SMS administration includes create, test and deploy SMS packages for applications and security patches.
- Provide GPO Administration for create, test and deploy GPO for desktop applets and or security updates.
- Provide Handheld Device and PDA administration to support all firm sanctioned PDA.

- Provide support for TWP sub-tenants: responsibilities include but are not limited to setting-up equipment, configuring and performing data backups; addressing data security and mail issues on a variety of Linux and BSD platforms.

Requirements

- Associates degree in Computer Science, Information Systems or comparable experiences.
- Experience offering Technical Support at an Investment Banking or comparable Financial Institution.
- Proficiency in (but not limited to) the following industry standard applications Bridge, Bloomberg, Lava, Bear Prime/WebShell, Fidelity StreetScape, Factset, DealMaven Applications.
- Ability to demonstrate proactive approach to problem resolution, strong troubleshooting and problem solving skills.
- Excellent knowledge of Microsoft Windows, and strong functional proficiency in the Microsoft Office Suite.
- Multimedia and security application software.
- Excellent interpersonal skills with ability to diplomatically address users' technical issues and problems.
- Ability to multi-task – address multiple and occasionally conflicting priorities in a in a fast paced environment.
- Possess excellent written and verbal communication skills.

Recommended Certifications

C014, C018, C019, C020, C021, C111

J097 IT Testing Engineer

Description

- Coordinate IT testing for systems and to ensure compliance to system specifications.
- Organize and coordinate Quality Assurance (QA) test suites for the verification of software applications.
- Design reviews, participating in the design of test plans, create test specifications, design, develop, maintain & execute test suites, document product defects, analyze and resolve regression tests.
- Work closely with the development team to ensure issues' resolutions in a timely manner.

Requirements

- Experience in testing client-server applications with a heavy reliance on performance, scalability and reliability.
- Experience testing applications in a highly regulated industry.
- Operational experience with MS SQL Server, Windows Operating Systems and MS Office, Mac OS.
- Ability to work independently with minimal supervision in a fast paced and rapidly changing environment.
- Organized, process oriented and communication/writing skills.

Requirements (Desired)
- Bachelors Degree.
- Exposure to Mac OS, Apple Script, HTML, UNIX and/or Shell.

Recommended Certifications
C103, C129

J098 Java Software Engineer

Description
- Develop, Unit Testing, System Testing, Implementation of EJB components, payment scrubbing rules and exception processing facility.

Requirements
- Software Engineer experience.
- Experience with Oracle, UNIX, EJB, Java and SDLC.

Recommended Certifications
C100, C102, C138,

J099 Lead or Manager, Software Engineering

Description
- Develop and deploy of complex Web applications.
- Work as a manager of an energetic and fast-paced web team implementing mission critical applications and following through on the deployment.
- Technical leadership to junior engineers, tracking deliverables, and coordinating testing.

Requirements
- BSc in Computer Science.
- Experience with high traffic web applications using Oracle with Java programming. As well as Strong background with Object-oriented design and implementation and relational database.
- Experience with large scale, high performance systems.
- Experience leading a team of developers.
- Good communication skills.

Recommended Certifications
C100, C102, C114, C138, C141

J100 Lead UNIX TCP/IP engineer

Description
- Lead server-side engineering team.
- Build and debug multi-threaded UNIX server software.

Requirements
- Experience building UNIX-based networking software.
- Experience with TCP/IP networking.

- A strong work ethic and good communication skills.

Recommended Certifications
C006, C018, C021

J101 Member Technical Staff-Senior Software Engineer

Description
- Develop innovative technologies, prototypes, components, processes and/or algorithms or develop new business opportunities.
- Solving complex problems, creating technical innovations, acting independently or with little supervision and serving as a liaison internally (technical and business development staff) and externally (clients, prospective clients and other interested parties).
- Involve in the areas of Leadership, Administration and Business Development as it relates to their particular business area.
- Complete life cycle development of software in a product development environment (software system and architecture design, software design and coding and test and documentation).

Requirements
- BSc in Computer Science.
- Experience developing commercial software products for technical application, including object oriented design and development.
- Strong skills in C++, Visual C++, MS Windows, MS Visual Studio.NET, MFC, GUI Programming and Visual Basic.
- Excellent communication verbal/written/listening and organizational skills. Also experienced group speaker/presenter.

Requirements (Desired)
- Strong skills in Java, J2EE, EJB, J2ME, Web Services, RMI, XML, Swing, JSP, JMS, JMF.
- Experience in databases, image/video processing and SEI.
- Experience in managing projects and/or tasks.

Recommended Certifications
C056, C100, C102, C114, C116, C118, C119, C120, C126, C127

J102 Messaging Engineer

Description
- Manage technical aspects of high volume email campaigns, estimating server and network capacity requirements.
- Recommend, plan for implementing server hardware/software upgrades in IIS Web farm to support email campaign requirements.
- Automate systems monitoring tasks using standard monitoring tools. As well as manage corporate inbound and outbound mail, including virus scanning and spam tools.

- Work with development teams on architecture of mail delivery platforms. Also communicate with other departments on email campaign requirements.
- Ensure the development and use of an effective preventive maintenance program suitable to meet the operation objective.
- Assist in management of corporate DNS and Active Directory infrastructure as well managing and optimizing email systems.
- Assist in planning, designing and implementing a high quality production environment as well assist in evaluating, recommending, and selecting equipment, services and vendors.
- Maintain and update documentation of the computing environment.
- Travel to datacenters for the deployment of the server architecture.
- Take part in on-call rotation and participate in 24x7 issue response, escalation and resolution.

Requirements
- Experience in system administration, server build and server troubleshooting, monitoring and troubleshooting, administrative scripting in VBScript, JavaScript or another scripting language, software/hardware standards and documentation standards.
- Experience in a large scale mission-critical production environment using MS web technologies (Windows, .NET and IIS, SQL Server).
- Expert knowledge in SMTP, Sendmail, Ironport SMTP appliance or similar technology, LAN/WAN technologies, TCP/IP networking and troubleshooting in a MS Windows networking environment, Compaq/HP server hardware, SAN and business suite management software, MS Active Directory, LDAP and security.
- Familiarity with UNIX systems (Linux/RedHat & Solaris) and ability to provide basic support on those platforms.

Requirements (Desired)
- Experience with ASPX/HTML.
- Fluent in at least one scripting language (JavaScript or VB Script).

Recommended Certifications
C004, C005, C006, C007, C014, C017, C018, C020, C103, C116, C122, C123, C127, C129, C132, C147, C149

J103 Network Engineer

Description
- Install and monitoring the MS Exchange Servers and Network.
- Assist in infrastructure management including SMS.

Requirements
- WAN/LAN analyst experience and network engineer experience.
- Experience with MS-Exchange and NT Server.
- SMS or Subnet, TCP/IP, NT Certification.

Requirements (Desired)
- Data communication engineer experience.

Recommended Certifications

C003, C004, C005, C006, C007, C018, C021

J104 Operations Analyst

Description

- Provide vendor management support for a large NT/PC network.

Requirements

- Technical support specialist experience.
- Knowledge of WAN and LAN.
- Business and project/vendor management.
- Knowledge of PC leasing, PC maintenance, and NT administration.

Recommended Certifications

C016, C018

J105 Oracle/Java Programmer Analyst

Description

- Provide full life cycle development of broadband provisioning systems to include customer support and warranty repair.
- Assist in raising the skill level of the employees assigned to the project.

Requirements

- Programmer Analyst experience.
- Experience with Oracle, Java and OJT techniques.

Requirements (Desired)

- Knowledge of telecom provisioning systems, broadband telecommunications and provisioning techniques.
- Knowledge of broadband telecom equipment.

Recommended Certifications

C100, C101, C102, C138, C141

J106 Oracle Software Engineer

Description

- Develop, maintain, Implement and provide user support to internal applications using Oracle development suite.
- Investigate new release of Oracle development suite in conjunction with Project Operations team to determine upgrade schedule and new enhancements on existing internal Oracle-based applications.
- Provide production and user support. Research & Analysis.
- Perform quality assurance work as assigned.
- Performs other business activities as necessary.

Requirements

- Bachelor's degree.

- Working knowledge in using Oracle development suite on Windows environment.
- Working knowledge of Oracle Finance, TCP/IP and Linux.
- Working knowledge of Sun, Solaris and UNIX.

Recommended Certifications

C004, C017, C138, C141, C149

J107 Perl Software Engineer

Description

- Develop, including high-level design/architecture, implement, and maintain of various web services.
- Communicate with a small group of software engineers and system administrators.
- Help in software development as moving to the next level of scalability and reliability.

Requirements

- BSc or advanced degree in Computer Science or a related field.
- Excellent knowledge of Perl, OO design and Linux/UNIX.
- Strong experience with all aspects of the software lifecycle, including testing and QA.
- Proficiency in Perl, Apache, Linux, SQL/MySQL, JavaScript, OOP, JavaScript and CSS.
- Experience coding web-based software applications.
- Architectural design experience with web-based software systems.
- Experience working on large-scale software systems or extremely high traffic web sites.

Recommended Certifications

C017, C103, C114, C122

J108 Real-Time Embedded Software Engineer

Description

- Involve the development and implementation of software for a broad range of real-time embedded signal processor systems.
- Utilize software engineering principles to design, code, debug, and implement software realizations of real-time digital signal processing algorithms.

Requirements

- MSc or BSc in Computer Engineering, Computer Science or Electrical Engineering with related experience.
- Depth understanding of object-oriented design.
- Familiarity with parallel processor systems, digital signal processing, and real-time operating systems.
- Able to work in a team environment.

Recommended Certifications

C019

J109 Real-Time Software Development Engineer

Description

- Real-time system software development and maintenance of a next-generation national aviation weather system.
- Real-time development will occur with custom in-house software as well as commercial off-the-shelf products.
- Participate in a team environment to design, develop and integrate a web based display implemented in DHTML/AJAX as well as infrastructure writer in Perl, Java and C/C++.

Requirements

- Bachelor's degree in Computer Science, Electrical Engineering, Physics, Applied Mathematics, System Engineering, or equivalent.
- Web application programming experience or related coursework.
- Experience with Java Advanced Imaging, XML, Log4j, JUnit, Ant, middleware, web services and web server administration.
- Understanding of software engineering methodology, experience with object-oriented analysis and design.
- Ability to work well in a dynamic team environment where individual effort matters and excellent oral and written communication skills.

Requirements (Desired)

- Knowledge of the Linux operating system.

Recommended Certifications

C056, C100, C102, C108, C119, C122

J110 Sales Support Engineer

Description

- Work closely with business development and sales as a technical consultant of ThinkFree's Server Edition and Desktop Edition products during sales calls, demonstrations, and lab tests.
- Build and maintain a close relationship with customers (Worldwide) and sales reps and the engineering team.
- Answer technical questions and conducts demonstrations of products and new features to prospects and to various groups within existing customer accounts.
- Provide product installation problem resolution and support. Also, provide full technical training of ThinkFree's products.
- Coordinate both technical and business issues between customers and engineers to meet customers' needs.
- Gather ongoing prospect/customer feedback, enhancement requests, and related information.
- Take part in tradeshows, conferences and marketing events.
- Provide hands-on technical assistance and troubleshooting support for customers. Also occasional travels to visit customers.

Requirements
- BSc in a computer and Internet subject.
- Experience as a sales engineer or system engineer in a mix of UNIX/Windows environment.
- Hands-on Linux/UNIX, Windows, and Mac OS experience.
- Knowledge of HTML, XML, Java, CGI, TCP/IP, HTTP, HTTPS, SSL, DMZ, etc.
- Outstanding account management and follow-through skills.
- Excellent ability to work closely with customers in pre- and post-sales situations also excellent communication skills.

Requirements (Desired)
- Experience providing application/network support and explaining technology to customers and sales prospects or providing internal support to company employees.
- Ability to interact with many different types of individuals, including executives, scientists, engineers, analysts, and other computer and business professionals.
- A broad background and general knowledge of technical, administrative, and financial areas, and a basic understanding of related terms and business processes.
- Knowledge of SQL and relational databases.

Recommended Certifications
C005, C014, C018, C021, C056, C100, C102,

J111 Senior Application Engineer

Description
- Perform as an Application Architect for the product suite.
- Provide technical leadership in design/implementation/development/support of application modules using Java and C++.

Requirements
- Degree in Computer Science.
- Enterprise product development experience.
- Experience with JBOSS, WebLogic, J2EE standards, Java, and UNIX scripting language.
- In-Depth experience in multi-tier client server architecture.
- Developed/implemented large scale multi-tier enterprise application or package solution.
- Outstanding track record in enterprise-level full life cycle applications development.
- Strong knowledge in Databases, Application and UI layers and their best practices, SQL, Relational databases and Oracle database.
- Strong understanding of OO development methodology.
- Worked at Enterprise level to address issues such as application performance, security, concurrency, cashing, state management, error handling, etc.
- Knowledge in CCTV industry.
- Perform independently and guide, assist or mentor others in analyzing, designing, coding, testing, debugging, documenting, and installing a large/complex or several smaller solutions.

Recommended Certifications
    C020, C100, C102, C114, C138, C141

J112 Senior Business Intelligence Analyst

Description
- Develop reporting and analytic solutions for business users based on business requirements.
- Participate in design of data warehouse/data marts to provide efficient and flexible reporting.
- Train and support end users on reporting/OLAP capabilities.
- Develop enterprise dashboards to enable management of critical business metrics.

Requirements
- Bachelor's degree and preferred in Computer Science.
- Experience in data warehousing and enterprise reporting.
- Experience with BI tools like Microstrategy or Business Objects.
- Strong knowledge of DW architecture and Oracle SQL.
- Flexible, and possess the ability to manage diverse personalities.
- Excellent problem solving skills and good communications.

Recommended Certifications
    C014, C114, C138, C141

J113 Senior Communications Engineer (VOIP)

Description
- Help design and install internal/external VOIP networks.
- Assist in the development and maintenance of network and voice communications as well as perform a variety of Converged VoIP Networking and IT related tasks.
- Test and evaluate Voice network systems to eliminate problems and make improvements.

Requirements
- Bachelor's degree, college technical degree or Filed Experience.
- Aptitude to learn quickly.
- 3Com NBX Systems Install.
- Cisco CCNA, and CCDA Certification.
- 3Com NBX or higher certification.
- Able to drive and service business customers at their location.

Requirements (Desired)
- Experience with all 3Com Network Equipment.
- Experience with APC rack and Power Protection Solution.
- Familiar and knowledgeable of FortiNet, Sonicwall, and Symantec.
- Working experience with Visio and MS Project.

Recommended Certifications
    C001, C004, C005

J114 Senior Database Engineer/Architect

Description
- Design, development and testing of the company's data warehouse as well as design and development of business level reporting.
- Design and implement a flexible data integration framework to integrate data from various distributed system in massive volume.
- Schema design for complex, high performance, large scale business analytics application.
- Monitor database performance and implement optimizations at the query, design, and configuration levels.
- Develop/deploy internal monitoring and reporting tools. Also create scripts and procedures for performing bulk database operations.
- Integration with OLTP system for optimal business practice.

Requirements
- BA or BSc in a relevant discipline and/or highly work experience.
- Professional experience working with MySQL and/or other major DBMS, database development, database design, SQL, stored procedure coding, database tuning and performance optimization.
- Experience with data loading and data transformation (ETL), source code control (preferably CVS) and some database administration.
- Work in high volume, high availability commercial environments developing and maintaining databases that power web applications.
- Proficient in various languages like Perl, Java.
- Good interpersonal and communication skills.

Requirements (Desired)
- Data warehouse design and development experience.
- Experience with web analytics software and website traffic analysis.

Recommended Certifications
C014, C019, C100, C102, C110, C113, C114, C119, C129, C138

J115 Senior DHTML/JavaScript Engineer – Consultant

Description
- Build a well-engineered, world-class user interface using DHTML, JavaScript, and Perl.
- Take ownership of the technical architecture of the project.
- Meet regularly with marketing and other customers to help determine project requirements.
- Work closely and brainstorm with other development team members. Also communicate clearly with company management.

Requirements
- Expert-level, experience with DHTML, JavaScript, Perl, CGI/HTTP and object oriented language, such as C++ or Java.

- Strong SQL and database/schema design skills.
- Ability to deliver solid, well-engineered code–thoroughly designed, documented, and tested.
- Demonstrated experience in product vision and ownership.
- Ability to accurately and aggressively determine time estimates and stay within those estimates.
- Highly self-motivated and excellent communication.
- Led the development of a project or product.

Recommended Certifications
C100, C102, C103, C108, C114, C129

J116 Senior Embedded Software Engineer

Description
- Serve as team member and expert consultant on a software development and maintenance team.
- Work on software that supports the collection and tracking of real-time flight information.
- The information is stored currently on an Oracle database and being moved to another type of database and is accessible throughout the command via the web.
- Perform tasks in accordance with the organization's programming standards and procedures.

Requirements
- Bachelor's degree in Engineering, Computer Science, or related field of study.
- Experience with embedded software development and C/C++ programming, MS Windows, MS office and UNIX-based systems.
- Experience with VxWorks programming.
- Experience with software configuration management.
- Experience and working knowledge in all phases of a software development lifecycle.
- Willing to take instruction and guidance from customer's engineers when determining technical solutions.
- Excellent written, verbal and presentation communication skills.

Requirements (Desired)
- Experience with Data Acquisition Systems.

Recommended Certifications
C019, C120, C138

J117 Senior IT Programmer Analyst

Description
- Understand business requirements through interactions with functional work teams and/or IT business analysts and then help translate these requirements into appropriate business application solution strategies.
- Design, develop, configure, and test Business application.

- Provide daily technical and consultative support to the business users of these applications.
- Develop operational and management reports per business requirements. As well Work with the projects managers and Business analysts in implementing projects per planned schedule.

Requirements
- BSc in Software Engineering, Information Systems or Business Administration.
- Strong technical analysis and software engineering skills with a solid background in order Management/financial systems.
- Experience with developing relational data management applications, implementing cross functional business application packages and technical configuration and data base administration for packaged applications.
- Experience with scripting and integration between multiple systems.
- Ability to provide necessary consultation, problem management, technical support and database administration for installed applications to ensure their availability and usability.
- Ability to effectively communicate status and plans to project managers or team leads and follow IT change management control processes and provide appropriate documentation as necessary.
- Ability to prepare configuration design documents, both individually and as part of larger groups, for software applications implementation.
- Willingness to learn new business processes/technology and a strong personal orientation to business partnership, customer service and quality.

Requirements (Desired)
- Experience with Microsoft Dynamics (Great Plains).
- Experience with .NET and/or Web Services.

Recommended Certifications
C014, C019, C110, C113, C119, C125, C126

J118 Senior Java Engineer

Description
- Design, create, and modify applications software or specialized utility programs. As well as design software or customize software with the aim of optimizing operational efficiency.
- Provide technical guidance to product management teams to develop product requirements documents.
- Analyze product requirements to produce technical requirements and technical design documentation.
- Analyze and design databases within an application area, working individually or coordinating database development as part of a team.

Requirements
- Experience with AJAX, Apache, Tomcat, JBOSS Application Server, Hibernate, XML, XSLT, SQL & UNIX, PHP, design and implementation of Java/J2EE web applications and building Web UI Components using JSP, JSTL, and JavaScript.

- Expert level knowledge of Java and J2EE including EJB.
- Strong HTML/DHTML skills, including multi-platform support, CSS, and JavaScript, UML, and debugging and problem solving skills.
- Experience with at least one of the following databases: PostgreSQL, MySQL, Oracle or/and DB2.
- Strong working knowledge of build and source code control tools (ant, CVS). Also familiarity with Perl, shell scripting, or Python.
- Experience developing in UNIX/Linux environments.
- Discipline to document ideas and code in a clear, comprehensive and organized manner.
- Experience in online advertising (search marketing and optimization, analytics, data retrieval and storage).
- Ability to work in a small team in a demanding, fast-paced, start-up environment and self-motivated and enthusiastic attitude.

Recommended Certifications

C017, C021, C026, C030, C032, C056, C061, C062, C069, C100, C102, C103, C108, C114, C129, C138

J119 Senior/Lead Software Engineer

Description

- Comfortable with an entrepreneurial management style and the need to be extremely flexible in order to compete.
- Build world class software that services the real needs of business customers.
- Want to be a part of an energetic and focused start-up that is bringing new technology and services to an emerging marketplace.

Requirements

- BSc or higher degree in Computer Science or related technical discipline.
- Experience with J2EE, UML, XML, Oracle DB, SQL, Adobe imaging technology, Adobe PDF, Java development, Solaris and NT/windows/XP platforms, Web Services and Web Applications.
- Deep knowledge of web services and enterprise applications.
- Strong system integration and business analysis experience.
- Strong knowledge of object oriented methodologies.
- Excellent communication skills.

Recommended Certifications

C014, C019, C056, C021, C100, C102, C103, C108, C116, C119, C122, C129, C138, C141

J120 Senior Network Security Engineer

Description

- Responsible for the overall security administration of information systems. In addition, support testing and troubleshooting of LAN and WAN security, including vulnerability analysis.

- Technical and project lead for design, upgrade and maintenance of firewalls, intrusion detection systems, and other network security hardware and software.
- Consult on the use of network protocols and applications with respect to security implications.
- Monitor security of systems (review logs, password usage, etc); notify management of any issues, and implement solutions.
- Write security policies, procedures and reports.

Requirements
- Network engineer experience and LAN administrator experience.
- Experience with UNIX, LAN, WAN, MQSeries, Veritas and information security.
- In-depth knowledge of networking protocols (TCP/IP suite).
- In-depth knowledge of information security protocols.

Recommended Certifications
C003, C004, C005, C006, C007, C009, C018, C020, C098, C099

J121 Senior Operations Engineer

Description
- Lead the design and implementation of the system and network infrastructure.
- Support the system information and electronic commerce systems.

Requirements
- Database administrator experience.
- UNIX systems administrator experience.
- Experience with Oracle and UNIX Administration.
- Experience with Java, JavaScript, Perl Scripting and TCP/IP.

Recommended Certifications
C005, C006, C014, C018, C100, C102, C110, C112, C113, C138, C141

J122 Senior Search Software Engineer - IR

Description
- Role in one or more of the following areas: information retrieval, text classification, machine learning, collaborative filtering and data mining.

Requirements
- BSc in Computer Science.
- Experience with in-house, open source or commercial IR systems.
- Experience with large scale, high performance systems, SQL, Oracle, JDBC, J2EE application servers, Java, JSP and Servlets.
- Experience with high traffic, database-driven web applications.
- Strong background with object-oriented design and implementation.
- Strong background in relational database design.
- Good communication skills.

Requirements (Desired)
- Significant research experience in information retrieval, machine learning, or a related field.
- Demonstrated contribution to a large-scale web search or e-commerce application and strong background in statistics.
- Experience leading a team of developers.

Recommended Certifications
C014, C019, C100, C102, C112, C114, C129, C138, C141

J123 Senior Server Engineer

Description
- Manage individual project teams of engineers.
- Write technical specifications as required in order to meet the objectives of functional specifications as well specify and, identify specific interfaces, methods, parameters, procedures or functions.
- Assist the Projects Engineers in the development of the functional specification of client projects. As well interact with Interactive Engineers on integration of presentation and server components.
- Deliver development assignments on time, within budget and high quality and provide time estimates on the development of modules.
- Ensure specific portions of the application meet the goals and specified functionality of a given project as defined in the functional and technical specifications.
- Assist in the development of the Engineering Architecture Quality Assurance Plan, Deployment Guide, Operations Guide and Engineering Technology assessments.
- Develop server-side modules of the application according to specifications using Java.
- Perform unit testing of all modules and participate in code reviews.

Requirements
- Bachelor's degree in Computer Science or equivalent.
- Experience with Java and OO programming, BEA, WebSphere, Dynamo, JBoss, CMS (Interwoven, Vignette, Percussion or Rhythmyx), version control, issue tracking, and build/release management.
- Familiarity with J2EE Application architecture, JDBC, EJB, JNDI, JMS, JSB, Struts, Tiles, JSF, Oracle, SQL Server, MySQL, SQL and UNIX based OS/Windows platforms.
- Understanding of application development concepts and design patterns and iterative development methodologies.
- Understanding of scripting (HTML, JavaScript, DHTML, etc) and its relationship to server side engineering components.
- Basic understanding of HTTP, DNS, and related network protocols.
- Prior experience in professional services industry.
- Good problem solving skills, excellent communication skills.

Recommended Certifications

C012, C019, C021, C025, C028, C029, C041, C042, C051, C055, C087, C100, C102, C103, C107, C108, C114, C129, C138, C141

J124 Senior Solutions Engineer

Description

- Partner with software sales professionals in the delivery of products, services, consulting and related activities to customers.
- Lead and deliver technical portion of sales presentations.
- Provide onsite technical information in support of sales transactions.
- Participate in seminars, road shows, conferences and user groups.
- Technically qualify (or disqualify) a prospective customer.

Requirements

- BSc in Computer Science/Computer Engineering or equivalent experience.
- Experience in IP networking-related product development.
- Strong understanding of IP protocols and networking industry.
- Experience in network security technologies.
- Excellent communication, interpersonal, and presentation skills.

Recommended Certifications

C005, C006, C007, C014, C018, C020

J125 Senior Software Engineer

Description

- Design, implement, and maintain modules within a large enterprise application.
- Integrate with external applications such as MS Word.
- The code is primarily in Java with heavy use of XML.
- Able to write components that both scale and perform.

Requirements

- Programming experience.
- Experience in web-based, server-side application development.
- Experience with Java and XML-related technologies (SAX, DOM, Xpath, XSLT, XSD, etc).
- Experience in enterprise application development demonstrated.
- Ability to pick up on and solve problems with new technologies self-starter and good communication skills.

Requirements (Desired)

- Familiarity with J2EE technologies, Word, PDF output technologies.
- Experience in COM, .NET, IIS, JBOSS.

Recommended Certifications

C056, C100, C101, C102, C108, C118, C122, C125, C126, C150

J126 Senior Staff Engineer

Description
- Client/Server programming using C and C++ in Linux environment.
- Develop applications including: text messaging, e-Commerce, and personalized services.
- Lead conversations with large groups to resolve complex engineering problems that span multiple disciplines and organizations. As well as be a team builder and team leader.

Requirements
- College degree or unfinished degree if possess vast self taught knowledge.
- Lead developer experienced.
- Experience with Client/Server programming using C and C++ in Linux environment.
- Experience with low level socket programming and TCP/IP.
- Comprehensive knowledge and development experience with a wide variety of mobile Internet technologies is essential.
- High intellectual capacity to deal with very complex problems.

Recommended Certifications
C005, C014, C017, C018, C019

J127 Senior Usability Engineer

Description
- Plan, design, and conduct usability evaluations such as task analysis, usability tests, heuristic evaluations, field studies, contextual inquiry, and competitive analyses during all phases of product development - both domestically and internationally.
- Determine and implement the usability methods/techniques that will yield the most effective data in a compressed development cycle.
- Oversee the development of the usability lab.
- Work with marketing and product to identify user segments and create user profiles.
- Analyze data, write reports, and present findings to cross functional teams. In addition, rapidly prototype features for testing.
- Evaluate and communicate results of studies and work with designers to come up with design solutions that solve the usability issues, adhere to site standards, and meet the business needs.

Requirements
- Graduate degree in Experimental Psychology, Cognitive Psychology, Human Computer Interaction or Human Factors, or other related discipline with a solid foundation in research design.
- Industry experience conducting usability research.
- Prior experience leading a team of usability engineers.
- Experience collectively working with user interface designers.

- Ability to rapidly prototype designs using an internet technology (HTML, Dreamweaver, Flash, etc).
- Experience in usability testing of web-based applications and conducting usability test internationally.
- Ability to work in a team environment as well self-driven, motivated, and willing to work under minimal supervision.

Recommended Certifications

C019, C103, C105, C106, C107

J128 Senior Web Programming Analyst

Description

- Web based development in support of the Lead Free application used in DSL provisioning.
- Responsibilities include development, data analysis and technical problem resolution.

Requirements

- Programmer analyst experience.
- Experience with Java, HTML, ColdFusion, PL/SQL and Oracle.

Requirements (Desired)

- Business analyst experience.

Recommended Certifications

C014, C100, C102, C103, C104

J129 Senior Wireless Software Engineer

Description

- Develop both client and server side components of products.
- Perform core coding and development on wireless products for several carriers and a wide range of mobile handsets.
- Be a key member of a software development team responsible for software development of mobile games and lifestyle applications.
- Coordinate with the QA team for product testing and bug fixes.
- Adhere to defined coding standards, defined quality standards and project development processes including documentation, defect tracking, software configuration management, status reporting and QA processes.

Requirements

- BSc in engineering or related subject.
- Software development experience in wireless industry.
- Experience with J2ME, BREW, WAP, SMS, entertainment software and application testing and debugging.
- Solid understanding of software development processes, including software design and documentation standards.
- Excellent written communication skill and comfortable working both individually and as part of a team.

Recommended Certifications
  C019

J130 Software Systems/Development Engineer

Description
- Define, design, and develop system requirements.
- Evaluate potential system architectures; define system specifications, input/output processes and working parameters.
- Perform system simulations where appropriate, translate system requirements into software architecture, produce top down design using structured development processes, and integrate with custom designed hardware.
- The resulting design must be fully functional, testable, and maintainable.

Requirements
- BSc in Computer Science or related.
- Work experience in systems and development engineering.
- Well-structured software development methodology, with consistent adherence to software configuration control.
- Experience on hardware/software projects includes analysis of system requirements and architecture design.
- Experience with Linux and Windows operating systems; C, C++, scripting languages; multi-threaded applications; networking.
- Performing high-level design, integration, test, and transitioning into production. As well as understanding of the "big picture".
- Ability to convey software system requirements to a small team of engineers, as well as to a subcontractor is a necessity.

Recommended Certifications
  C017, C019, C123

J131 Software Application Engineer

Description
- Design, develop, test, and support software products for an OEM device.
- Develop, implement, and maintain application level software.
- Develop products following company SOP's.
- Participate in design and code reviews, and communicate technical concepts clearly and effectively both verbally and in writing.
- Obtain an in-depth working knowledge of products and targeted users.
- Work with development team to write design specifications.

Requirements
- Relevant degree (CS, EE or CE is preferred).
- Software engineering experience.
- Experience with C#, C/C++ or other relevant languages, .NET, XML and object oriented design techniques with a commitment to quality.

- Experience using debugging tools, software source control and issue tracking systems.

Requirements (Desired)
- Familiarity with ISO/FDA regulations.

Recommended Certifications
C056, C108, C122, C125, C127

J132 Software Engineer

Description
- Produce high quality code that is reliable, extensible and scalable, using Microsoft Technologies, to build or improve highly sophisticated applications that are founded on intricate business logic, while complying with project standards and quality levels.
- Respecting challenging deadlines, in a interwoven, mind stimulating, skill sharpening, self energizing, fun and lively environment built by an ever growing visionary company.

Requirements
- Expert level working knowledge of COM, DCOM, COM+, XML, ASP, VBScript, JavaScript, IIS, VB and HTML.
- Expert level working knowledge of intricate SQL statements, MS SQL keys, triggers, stored procedures and views.
- Working knowledge of Visual Studio, Visual Interdev, and Visual Source Safe.
- Expert understanding and ability working with highly complex Logic and excellent communication skills and strong attention to detail.

Recommended Certifications
C056, C108, C114, C116, C118, C119, C122

J133 Software QA Engineer

Description
- Plan, design, and execute testing for application and system infrastructure components and subsystems.
- Create automation test suite and requisite infrastructure as needed.
- Work closely with development engineers and project managers to execute testing, report, and track defects, according to PDLC schedule. Also develop and document test plans and procedures.
- Participate in design and development of test approach per project.
- Execute, analyze, document test results, and work closely with the developers to isolate and reproduce defects.
- Participate in technical design and code reviews.
- Interact closely with members of the cross-functional team.

Requirements
- BSc or MSc in Computer Science or equivalent.
- Understanding of OO programming and relational DB concepts.

- Experience with Perl, Python, and/or UNIX Shell scripting and Linux with working knowledge of web-based application protocols.
- Solid background on Apache, Solaris/Linux, HTTP/CGI, HTML, XML, XSLT, etc.
- Hands-on application-level experience with SQL databases (prefer Oracle) and significant scripting/programming experience.
- Understanding of multi-user software development and ability to read and understand technical design specification documents.
- Ability to design test plans and execute test procedures for complex applications as well as troubleshooting and debugging.
- Passion for QA and excellent written/verbal communication skills.

Requirements (Desired)
- Good knowledge of QA methodology, including L&P.
- Experience developing database applications.
- Programming experience with C++/Java.
- Experience with troubleshooting in UNIX environment.
- Experience designing/implementing automatic test harnesses.
- Experience with data-driven, white box test automation & system-level testing.

Recommended Certifications
C017, C056, C100, C101, C102, C103, C107, C108, C114, C122, C129, C138, C141, C150

J134 Systems Engineer

Description
- Support Windows operating systems, configuring and installing computer hardware and operating system software.
- Tune and validate Windows systems, troubleshooting and resolving problems and outages.
- Work extensively with development staff (all applications), and assist in resolution of hardware/software platform problems in complex, layered, client/server-based software.
- Assign system logon passwords and maintain software logs and system software installation media.
- Provide backups of available servers/software/applications.
- Manage electronic messaging and telephony components, as they pertain to the operating systems environment.
- Maintain library of documentation for system software.
- Understand strategic business continuance initiatives as keys to maintaining a high availability of IT services to reduce financial impact of downtime on product/customer cycle.
- Eliminate system downtime, respond to system failures in a timely way and monitor and test contingency planning processes and procedures.
- Anticipate problems and work closely with management to identify areas with risk potential.

- Implement standards and maintain a high level of user trust and confidence in the group's knowledge of and concern for users' business needs and the critical nature of seamless IT functioning for internal and external users.
- Frequently interact with third-party technology vendors and internal facilities staff.
- Interact with database staff (Oracle Database Administrators and System Programmers).

Requirements

- Bachelor's degree in Computer Science or other technical discipline, or related work experience.
- Microsoft Certified Systems Engineer.
- Experience in Systems Engineering.
- Extensive knowledge of Windows Server Platforms, various backup software platforms, various SAN and Storage Array Products.
- Detailed-oriented, self-motivated, able to work in a team and independently and excellent written/verbal communication skills.

Requirements (Desired)

- Experience with HP and Dell server hardware.

Recommended Certifications

C021, C083, C123, C129

J135 Technical Marketing Engineer

Description

- Perform detailed requirements analysis by discussing requirements with domain experts, line of business representatives, prospective users, and/or other individuals who could contribute requirements for the project.
- Create proof-of-concept models, diagrams and/or rapid prototypes of proposed solutions (including textual documentation) to enable project stakeholders to visually verify the business development team's current understanding of the project requirements.
- Travel as needed to provide technical project support and assistance.

Requirements

- BSc in Computer Science or equivalent combination of education and experience.
- Information technology development experience within storage industry including backup and recovery, disaster recovery software and/or hardware.
- Experience with Backbone, Computer Associates (CA), CommVault, EMC, Hitachi, HP-Compaq, Iron Mountain, Legato, LiveVault, MSI, StorageTek, Network Appliance, Tivoli, or Veritas.
- Experience administering, supporting, and configuring Operating Systems including: Solaris (Sun), Linux (RedHat), Netware (Novell), UNIX (IBM, HP) and MS Windows.
- Programming experience with Java, ODBC, SQL, Perl, CGI, HTML, XML, SOAP, .NET.
- Hardware experience with storage systems like archive systems, WORM, Magnetic/Optical Storage, RAID, NAS, and SAN's.

- Experience with critical data protection scenarios that may include disaster recovery, system restores, or data archiving.
- Ability to work as a team member in a fast-paced environment.

Recommended Certifications

C014, C017, C018, C034, C056, C081, C100, C102, C103, C107, C108, C122, C125, C126, C127, C129, C132, C137, C147, C149, C150

J136 Technical Operations Engineer

Description

- Hands-on position that includes the rack and stack of machines, cabling of machines, site documentation and basic OS installs.
- Responsible for Cabling, racking and configuring machines to customer specifications.
- Answering tickets and performing tasks as specified by the customer.
- Perform basic troubleshooting and read and follow Visio diagrams.
- Follow all procedures provided to complete tasks as noted in procedural documentation.

Requirements

- Basic understanding of computers, hardware and software.
- Familiarity with internal working of computer hardware, disks, CPU, memory and limited experience with multiple operating systems.
- Conceptually understand the Internet, data centers, circuits, routers, and firewalls.
- Experience in IT environments, customer support, help desk.
- Experience with MS Office or equivalent applications, RAID systems and ticketing systems.
- Experience installing, configuring, maintaining, and troubleshooting web servers.
- Have or be in the process of obtaining MCSE WIN2K.
- Able and willing to lift, carry, cable, un-box, etc.

Recommended Certifications

C005, C006, C007, C018, C123

J137 Visual Basic Programmer Analyst

Description

- Be a team member that Designs, Maintains and Administers in-house developed business application, developed in VB and SQL.
- Perform complex problem solving tasks with regards to application development and data analysis and messaging.
- Assist in implementing ideas and solutions to improve application and database performances, including Normalization Environment setups, Data migrations.
- Assist in implementing and merging new Business practices into application functionality.

Requirements

- Visual Basic programming in a Client/Server environment.

- Experience in SQL Server database design and development.
- Experience with SQL Scripting, advanced VB and advanced SQL.
- Detail oriented with great problem solving and debugging skills.
- Good communication skills, positive attitude and a Team Player.

Requirements (Desired)
- Experience with developing Crystal Reports and familiarity with Crystal Enterprise.
- Knowledge and experience with SQL Server Reporting and Data Warehousing.

Recommended Certifications
C108, C114, C116, C122, C129

J138 Web Data Analyst

Description
- Create, certify, and interpret web statistics with the objective of identifying trends.
- Support business analysis efforts, and provide information to support business decisions for the funds websites.
- Create reports utilizing NetGenesis and other available reporting tools, interpret reports requests and provide reports, and certify and validate report data.
- Spearhead the web analytical effort and developing long-term strategies, and work closely with website technical administrators to schedule reports and maintain the system.

Requirements
- Experience in web analytics with extensive knowledge of the NetGenesis products.
- A strong understanding of web and non-web data required to meet business reporting objectives.
- Micro strategy experience. As well as strong technical skills including SQL, web log processing and strong database skills.
- A proactive individual with strong oral/written communication, detail orientation skills. In addition, some travel is required.

Requirements (Desired)
- Mutual fund industry experience and a college degree.

Recommended Certifications
C014, C108, C112, C114, C122, C129

J139 Web Production Engineer

Description
- Develop, modify, maintain and administrate web-based applications and media projects.
- Develop CMS based site architecture, template and tools.
- Perform testing and functional verification of development projects from an engineering perspective.
- Ensure delivery of deliverables and projects on time.
- Establish front-end technology requirements.

Requirements

- Bachelor's degree in Engineering, Design, or related field coupled with relevant experience.
- Professional web development experience.
- Expert-level experience in creating/debugging HTML (hand coding), XHTML, CSS, DHTML, JavaScript, and XML.
- Experience with Oracle, MySQL, and SQL Server.
- Knowledge of JSP, Perl, PHP, ASP and Python.
- Expert knowledge of web standards, cross browser compatibility and usability.
- Experience working in service business environment.
- Ability to execute multiple, interdependent end to end projects.
- Organized and excellent oral/written communication skills.

Requirements (Desired)

- Experience with Macromedia Flash design and Action Script development.

Recommended Certifications

C014, C056, C100, C103, C105, C106, C107, C108, C114, C116, C119, C122, C129, C138, C141

CHAPTER

9 COMPUTER MANAGERS JOBS

Manager is a person who is responsible for directing and running an organization or project. The person or firm responsible for the planning, coordination and controlling of a project from inception to completion, meeting the project's requirements and ensuring completion on time, within cost and to required quality standards.

Sometimes referred to as the data warehouse project manager, the Project Manager has overall responsibility for a project's successful implementation. The Project Manager defines, plans, schedules, and controls the project. The project plan must include tasks, deliverables and resources – the people who will perform the tasks. The manager will monitor and coordinate the activities of the team, and will review their deliverables.

J140 Applications Development Manager

Description

- Manage and provide oversight for application developers who are involved in several simultaneous projects of differing sizes with diverse teams; manage day-to-day team workflow and high-level project schedule for senior management.
- Work with the e-commerce business team to identify and define system enhancements.
- Work with the System Architect to develop the application environment using Service Oriented Architecture.
- Assist w/strategic direction of Applications Development and Maintenance team.
- Coordinate across multiple project teams, assuring adherence to overall objectives and standards, supervise external vendors, and provide input to other related projects.
- Oversee ongoing maintenance and development of systems that support our daily enterprise-level operations.
- Take a leadership role in establishing sound application development practices throughout the organization.
- Communicate effectively within the IT Team and facilitate information sharing with CompuMentor staff and management.
- Carry out other management and technical duties.

Requirements

- Bachelors Degree or equivalent experience.
- Web application development including hands-on and analytical experience: work with commercial grade e-commerce web sites and systems, and enterprise-level processing systems.
- Well honed leadership, supervisory, planning and organization skills. As well as strong demonstrated teamwork skills.
- Solid understanding of business applications, web/internet applications, database technologies, and applications architecture.
- Ability to translate business requirements into technical solutions.
- Experience with .NET, Classic ASP, VB, COM, XML/XSLT, IIS, MS SQL Server, HTML, CSS, web services, e-commerce and MS Windows environment.
- Full software development lifecycle experience and enterprise application development and integration experience.

Requirements (Desired)

- Experience with one major ERP/CRM enterprise application.
- Experience with PHP/LAMP and (W3C WAI).

Recommended Certifications

C014, C019, C103, C107, C108, C109, C112, C114, C118, C119, C120, C122, C125, C126, C127, C128, C129, C142, C143, C144, C145

J141 Client Services Project Manager

Description
- Create, communicate, update, and execute the Client Implementation Plan. This involves routine client contact via written and verbal communication (telephone and web conferencing).
- Conduct and document Client Review Meetings at project launch and at various intervals throughout the Client implementation.
- Record and maintain client documentation through a series of written forms keeping accurate records of discussions, expectations, commitments and deliverables.
- Execute the implementation plan; perform the tasks required to meet deliverables outlined in the plan, working with various internal resources and third parties as necessary and provide guidance and best practices mentoring to the clients.
- Document the progress of the implementation plan, keeping track of completed and outstanding issues and activities and providing timely documentation along the way.
- Provide regular implementation status updates to management.

Requirements
- BA/BSc degree.
- Experience in managing projects for client software or service implementations preferably in eCommerce, payment processing or financial services markets.
- Strong analytical skills regarding technical, contractual and financial issues.
- Excellent knowledge of Microsoft Office applications (including Microsoft Project and Visio), Outlook and the Internet is required.
- Ability to maintain excellent customer relationships (both internal and external) and excellent follow-through skills.
- Excellent organizational and verbal/written communication skills.
- Flexible team player that is able to isolate, analyze and correct problems in a timely manner.

Recommended Certifications
C014, C112, C142, C143, C144, C145

J142 Content Manager

Description
- Define and coordinate the implementation of site content to enhance user experiences.
- Review and edit site content to ensure timeliness and relevance.
- Assist in the integration and deployment of third party data feeds and maintains relationships with all data providers, including updates, edits and reporting.
- Identify and recommend content opportunities to improve visitor and other site metrics.

Requirements
- Experience in managing content providers, online info/search industries and organizing data for end-user interfaces.

- Ability to work well with others, inside and outside the company.
- Able to meet deadlines within demanding, fast-paced environment.

Requirements (Desired)
- BA or BSc degree.

Recommended Certifications
C142, C143

J143 IT Project Manager

Description
- Determine appropriate products or services with clients and work with customers to define project scope, requirements, and deliverables.
- Develop, modify, or provide input to project plans.
- Implement project plans to meet objectives.
- Coordinate and integrate project activities.
- Manage, lead, or administer project resources.
- Monitor project activities and resources to mitigate risk.
- Implement or maintain quality assurance process.
- Make improvements, solve problems, or take corrective action when problems arise.
- Give presentations or briefing on all aspects of the project.
- Participate in phase, milestone, and final project reviews.
- Identify project documentation requirements and procedures; and develop and implement product release plan.
- Identify and analyze customers' information systems requirements.
- Evaluate, monitor, or ensure compliance with laws, regulations, policies, standards, or procedures.
- Ensure appropriate product-related training and documentation are developed and made available to customers.
- Advises other IT experts throughout the agency or in other agencies on a variety of situations and issues that involve applying or adapting new theories, concepts, principles, standards, methods, or practices, that are developed by the employee or result from the employee's leadership; and serves as senior expert and consultant to top agency management officials to advise on integrating IT programs with other programs of equivalent scope and complexity.

Requirements
- Specialized experience with the particular knowledge, skills, and abilities to perform successfully the duties of the position such as:
    - Analyzing information technologies, architecture, and standards.
    - Developing functional and technical requirements and specifications.
    - Establishing policies and procedures for the use, distribution and support of IT assets.
    - Evaluating and recommending new database technologies and architecture.

o   Defining and maintaining physical and virtual network architecture and in-
    frastructure.
o   Leading or managing computer projects.

Recommended Certifications
C018, C019, C114, C142, C143, C144, C145

J144 Linux Server Tech/Support Manager

Description
- Assist in managing and developing a Linux server support program for web hosting company.

Requirements
- Hands-on hardware installation experience (install drives, NIC, etc).
- Experience in managing, provisioning and securing multiple account Linux servers.
- Expertise in Linux server installations.
- Troubleshoot CGI, Perl, PHP, and MySQL support issues.

Requirements (Desired)
- Experience with Modernbill and cPanel preferred.

Recommended Certifications
C017, C019, C142

J145 Manager, Decision Support Systems

Description
- Report directly to the VP of Technology.
- Manage all phases of data warehouse development, including requirements gathering and prioritization.
- Develop the zipRealty report mart.
- Manage release dates and included functionality.
- Maintain quality assurance and quality measurement of data and data sources.
- Participate in the evaluation and selection of new technology.
- Provide technical support and consultation supports to users analyze business problems and suggest potential solutions.
- Coordinate with functional departments to collect system requirements.
- Maintain relationships with outside data content vendors.
- Ensuring that the information technology department supports all division and corporate business strategies.
- Define, implement, and support standards, policies, and procedures related to information technology.

Requirements
- BSc in business administration or other related major.
- Hands-on technical experience in the data warehouse and decision support disciplines.
- Comfortable with SQL and report generation tools and systems.
- Excellent organization skills, excellent people skills, and excellent team spirit.

Requirements (Desired)
- Information Technology management experience.

Recommended Certifications
C019, C114, C142

J146 Program Manager, Strategic Technology Programs

Description
- Manage high-priority strategic and tactical programs sponsored by the CTO working with all levels of management across Engineering, Operations and Quality Assurance.
- Ability to define, manage and deliver high visibility projects.
- Program focus will be in the areas of system architecture, financial systems and software development life cycle.

Requirements
- Bachelor's Degree or Equivalent.
- Solid experience managing technology programs.
- Professional certifications and continuing education history suggest knowledge of, adherence to, and commitment to project management practices.
- Disciplined technical project management experience in the internet or software industry with increasing demonstrated responsibility.
- Project management, process management skills.
- Able to form and drive a cross-functional team of leaders to: articulate program goals/vision, establish program roadmap, set delivery goals across teams and manage execution against a committed plan.

Requirements (Desired)
- Ability to significantly advance program management practices.
- Technical degree or experience as a software engineer.

Recommended Certifications
C019, C123, C142, C143

J147 QA Manager

Description
- Automate and manage the certification of a J2EE application.
- Support functionality, besides delivery of HTML, PDF, Excel, XML content over the web, includes repository (certified against different RDBMS), scheduling, security and directory services.

Requirements
- QA management experience.
- Experience with certification of web-based enterprise software.
- Experience with certification of standalone authoring tools.
- Experience with J2EE application servers (Tomcat, WebLogic, and WebSphere), operating systems (Windows, Linux and Solaris) and databases (Oracle, SQL Server, DB2, Sybase, and MySQL).

- Hands-on experience writing scripts for automation, using testing tools like SilkTest.

Recommended Certifications

C017, C019, C020, C021, C029, C050, C051, C055, C056, C058, C059, C060, C061, C069, C103, C107, C115, C118, C129, C138, C142

J148 Release Manager

Description

- Use established project management methodology/tools, develop and execute project plans, which include work plans, schedules, milestones, project scope and deliverable/responsibility matrices.
- Assist engineering teams in project planning, tracking, reporting, resource allocation, issues resolution, impact analysis, risk and change management.
- Manage project scope, resources, and timeline to ensure quality delivery, on time and within budget.
- Communicate project information to all project team members, sponsors, and vendors and escalating issues and risks to management when needed.
- Work closely with various departments (QA, Engineering, Technical Publications, Product Management, Support, Product Marketing, PSO, Pre-Sales) to coordinate timely release deliverables.
- Perform variance analysis (including schedule, costs vs. budgets, resources and changes to scope).

Requirements

- Degree in Computer Science or Equivalent.
- Experience in a software engineering environment, with experience in a project management/release management (or equivalent) role.
- Experience coordinating releases and managing staff.
- Knowledge of project planning methodologies.
- Ability to work within an internationally structured team.
- Strong skills in presentation and reporting, analytical, diagnostic and problem solving, and written/verbal communication.

Requirements (Desired)

- PMI or equivalent certification.
- Experience with Iterative Development, working with remote teams and improving processes.
- Exposure to Internet messaging protocols (SMTP, HTTP, DNS) and Wireless protocols (WAP, SyncM L).

Recommended Certifications

C019, C142, C145

J149 Search Manager

Description

- Perform in-depth quantitative analyses of marketing campaigns.

- Act as the face of the company to clients. As well ensure that all company products and services are meeting client goals.
- Develop, execute and monitor effective online marketing campaigns, specifically using search engines as the delivery vehicle for obtaining targeted leads and acquisitions.
- Develop and implement online search engine marketing strategies to achieve client goals. Also analyze and report customer data.
- Provide frequent progress reports regarding online marketing efforts and performance metrics to clients.
- Help clients achieve their goals by utilizing additional company products and services.

Requirements
- Bachelor's Degree.
- Online marketing experience including campaign development and performance analyses.
- Exceptional quantitative analytical skills and aptitude including intermediate to advanced Excel skills.
- Experience in a client-facing position (eg, account management, client management, and senior client support or business development).
- Strong software use skills including in-depth knowledge of Microsoft Office applications (Word, Excel, PowerPoint, Outlook, and Access), and aptitude to quickly learn new tools.
- Exceptional problem-resolution skills including the ability to think creatively in the development of ideas/solutions that will contribute value in a dynamic, client-centered environment.
- High comfort level utilizing the internet as a research and/or shopping tool.
- Ability to work well in a team, to shine as an individual and to handle multiple assignments with effective resolution. As well as excellent written/verbal communication skills.

Requirements (Desired)
- Direct experience in search engine marketing.
- Within online marketing experience, emphasis on analyzing performance and optimizing marketing campaigns.
- Strong technical aptitude including some ability to understand basic website programming language and basic financial analysis skills.

Recommended Certifications
C014, C019, C108, C142

J150 Senior Online Marketing Manager

Description
- Track, measure, and analyze the performance of all online marketing campaigns including PPC (keywords), paid inclusion, paid link and banner advertising and promotions.

- Analyze website visitor activity, interpret results and suggest ways to improve customer acquisition and conversion.
- Direct all paid search and paid inclusion campaigns, including optimization of search engine ads, landing pages, and bids.
- Work with outside providers to manage banner advertising creative development and media buys.
- Develop and execute link building and search box distribution strategies. In addition, manage campaign-testing processes - development and coordination of AB tests.
- Work with a cross-functional team to improve organic search results (SEO).

Requirements
- Bachelor's degree or equivalent work experience.
- Savvy online marketer with interactive marketing/advertising experience and direct experience in search engine optimization and managing bids.
- Experience with bid/keyword management tools or programmatically driven search engine marketing agencies.
- Experience with web analytics software (Hitwise, Websidestory).
- Skilled at analysis, data manipulation, and data presentation.
- Proficient with Excel, Word, PowerPoint.
- High level of energy and an enthusiastic team player.
- Work in a small team environment with excellent analytical, problem solving and written/verbal communication skills.

Recommended Certifications
C014, C019, C045

J151 Senior Project Manager

Description
- Manage multiple projects to a successful outcome consisting of a satisfied client and an on time, on-budget and on-specification project.
- Responsible for proposal and initial scope, schedule and budget documents used for sales and business development purposes.
- Formally gather, document, and communicate project requirements, specifications and progress.
- Track detailed budgets, schedules and tasks throughout the project's development.
- Statement of work, technical and user experience specifications project "builds", internal reviews, client project extranet, and end of project review and evaluation.
- Serve as the senior lead responsible for multi-disciplinary team consisting of content expertise areas such as client and server side engineering, database engineering, user experience, information architecture, visual design, and digital media.
- Manage external resources such contractors including contract discussions, contracts and contractor payments.
- Manage client deliverables such as project invoicing, client payments, client feedback, client approvals, and content and equipment requirements.

Requirements

- BSc/BA in Computer Science, Engineering, Communications, or Business Management.
- Experience with engineering technology.
- Ability to schedule, budget and delegate. As well able to understand and articulate full aspects of technical and creative development.
- Superior organization abilities particularly the ability to manage multiple projects simultaneously.
- Strong understanding and appreciation for client's business goals and ability to lead the process of translating those goals into tangible online presence; strategic experience.
- Hands-on development experiences also knowledge of Flash and enterprise technology standards and systems.
- Experience managing technology oriented projects in the internet development area, HTML and Photoshop.
- Capable of running a rich internet application development project from start to finish.
- Strong written/verbal communication skills.

Requirements (Desired)

- MBA.

Recommended Certifications

C014, C019, C045, C103, C106, C142, C143, C144, C145

J152 SEO Manager

Description

- Build and grow natural search distribution from the ground up.
- Effectively produce SEO solutions that result in achieving the top keyword rankings, on each of the leading search engines.

Requirements

- Ability to identify and secure the highest impact external links in the industry.
- Thorough understanding of the unique elements required to develop highly effective external link campaigns.
- Able to deliver work in HTML format, WYSIWYG is acceptable.
- Solid understanding of the role technology plays in getting pages fully indexed.
- Through knowledge of techniques necessary to improve click thru rates from natural search results.
- Highly effective content writer, able to produce highly effective copy that optimizes page conversions, while supporting SEO strategic goals. Also thorough understanding of "over optimization".
- High-conversion keywords based on limited exposure to target market analysis data.
- Excellent communication, organization and interpersonal skills.

Recommended Certifications

C019, C103

J153 Team Lead for .Net Project

Description
- Direct all activities required to design and to develop internet applications.
- Set schedules for completion of projects and write code.
- Estimate development effort and producing technical specifications.
- Interfacing with other managers to help provide consistency with the desktop product.

Requirements
- Degree in Computer Science or other technical field.
- Work experience in the mortgage industry.
- Thorough knowledge of .Net, .Net framework, Server Farm deployment, Visual Basic, SQL Server.
- Working knowledge of Com+/ActiveX, Oracle, Client-Server ntier.
- Ability to deliver high-quality internet products on a timely basis.

Recommended Certifications
C014, C019, C108, C122, C125, C129, C138

J154 Technical Consultant and Account Manager

Description
- Lead provider of strong digital identity solutions.
- Post sales deployments.

Requirements
- Deployment and project management experience.
- Worked experience in similar roles in an enterprise software.
- Able to provide good customer references.
- Experience in a technical implementation role in an enterprise software deployment.
- Understanding of the Enterprise Identity Management, Security market space and enterprise IT infrastructure.
- Familiar with both Windows and UNIX platforms, scripting languages, XML, directories, and security technologies.

Recommended Certifications
C020, C019, C056, C098, C115

J155 Technical Manager - Custom Software Development - .NET

Description
- Lead specification and documentation activities.
- Lead custom software design efforts.
- Lead custom software development efforts.
- Lead Q.A design plans and testing efforts.
- Lead implementation and post implementation efforts.

- Project estimates and ongoing work plans.
- Staff management and mentoring.

Requirements

- BSc in computer Science or equivalent.
- Experience with project management.
- Experience in custom software development consulting.
- Experience with Microsoft .NET Technologies.
- Strong understanding of custom development SDLC.
- Strong written/verbal communication skills.

Recommended Certifications

C019, C125, C126, C127, C145

CHAPTER

10 COMPUTER PROGRAMMERS JOBS

A programmer is a person who masters software engineering and writes source code in the course of software development. In language-oriented development, the programmer has to learn the details of the domain to be able to write a direct solution. In domain-oriented development, the programmer writes code for a generator instead of a direct solution.

J156 .NET Programmer

Description
- Work on comparable .NET projects.
- Able to program complex solutions in C#, utilizing the following technologies: .NET, SQL Server, XML/XSLT, and Web services.

Requirements
- Experience with object oriented concepts and programming.
- Intermediate to expert level C# knowledge.
- Highly proficient in programming to SQL server (Stored Procedures, ADO.NET, etc).
- Strong familiarity with .NET Web services requirements and functionality, and XML/XSLT.
- Experience in building both web and windows-based applications.
- Experience in web based application design and development.

Recommended Certifications
C056, C107, C108, C116, C117, C119, C120, C122, C125, C126, C127, C129

J157 C++ Programmer

Description
- Provide C++ and Java Bean programming support.

Requirements
- Programmer experience.
- Experience with Java, UNIX, C++, EJB and Java Beans.

Recommended Certifications
C100, C101, C102, C150

J158 Contract Web Programmer

Description
- Develop high-quality mathematics education applications including Geometer's Sketchpad and Fathom Dynamic Statistics Software.

Requirements
- College degree or equivalent.
- Advanced web application development experience in the area of user registration, management, reporting and administrative front-end to a web/DB backend.
- Experience with PHP, Perl, DBI, Mod_Perl, HTML, JavaScript, MySQL, and Apache Web server on Linux/UNIX.
- Ability to write clean/well documented code.
- Ability to work on a dedicated project and manage outcomes in conformance with organizational goals and objectives.
- Established record of providing innovative technical solutions.
- Ability to work both independently and as a member of a team.

- Excellent organizational, interpersonal and professional skills.

Recommended Certifications
C017, C103, C114, C117

J159 DB2 Programmer

Description
- Design, construct, test and deploy intersystem communication type applications.
- Use triggers and stored procedures within the DB2 environment.
- Participate in knowledge base transfer and production support issues with the Enterprise architects, Database administrators and other teams as well.

Requirements
- Database Developer experience.
- Experience with TSO, COBOL, DB2, JCL, OS and XML.
- Experience with DB2, FTP/XCOM, MSMQ and MQSeries

Requirements (Desired)
- Broker Technology.

Recommended Certifications
C026, C056, C060, C069, C114

J160 EDI Programmer

Description
- Maintain in-house EDI system and provide technical assistance for in-house and customer EDI system users.
- Install updates, expand, maintain, and troubleshoot EDI and accounting software.
- Resolve EDI and accounting network issues.

Requirements
- Bachelor's degree in Computer Science or related.
- Experience with EDI and accounting programming.

Recommended Certifications
C014, C112

J161 Java Application Programmer, Senior

Description
- Maintain and enhance of Information Management System (IMS).
- Work with system architects and product management to define, specify and review business/end-user requirements.
- Work with system architects to define and specify the architectural approach.
- Define technical requirements for assigned features and review technical requirements with other engineers.
- Develop functional specifications including technical implementation and review functional specifications created by other personnel.

- Design, develop, and debug UI and Server code for multiple components.
- Support QA department by reviewing test cases and applying bug fixes. Also recommend testing coverage and guidelines.
- Investigate and resolve issues in currently deployed product.
- Ensure that newly developed features meet performance, reliability, security, and scalability goals.
- Ensure successful deployment of given feature sets including meeting business requirements, UI/Server interface requirements, and overall product quality.
- Recode a Pascal like imaging program into Java.

Requirements
- An undergraduate degree.
- Experience with Visual Basic, Java, JSP, Struts, Tomcat, JavaScript, Pascal, Microsoft SQL Server (understanding schemas and SQL), Windows OS, MS-Office and Project management.
- Ability to work independently with minimal supervision in a fast paced and rapidly changing environment.
- Strong verbal/written communication skills and interpersonal skills.

Requirements (Desired)
- Experience with .NET, HTML and Crystal Reports.
- Knowledge of C, C++, Microsoft Access and Visual Source Safe.
- HL7 knowledge and experience, and HIPAA understanding.

Recommended Certifications
C012, C019, C100, C101, C103, C108, C114, C120, C125, C126, C127, C129, C150

J162 Macintosh Game Programmer

Description
- Response for the full life-cycle of projects, including requirements design, technical design, task estimation, implementation, automated testing, debugging, and deployment.
- Able to play well with others' in the development team and in the rest of the company.

Requirements
- BSc (or higher) in Computer Science.
- Experience professional software development.
- Experience C++ development.
- Experience with localized and cross-platform product development.
- Strong understanding of end-user experience.
- Experience with OpenGL and MacOSX GUI programming.
- Facility with object-oriented design and implementation.

Requirements (Desired)
- Experience implementing and deploying video games.
- Experience developing/deploying networked multiplayer games.
- Experience with DirectX and familiarity with relational databases.

Recommended Certifications
C114

J163 PHP Programmer

Description
- Develop new solutions using industry standard technologies with HTML, PHP, MySQL, and JavaScript.
- Perform quality control and security re-enforcements to gaming related features.
- Enhance existing code-base to conquer scalability problems or bottlenecks.
- Optimize database-driven functions involving enterprise level activities and updates.

Requirements
- Experience with PHP, MySQL and web development.
- Familiar with Linux, JavaScript and DHTML.
- Ability to keep abreast of current technologies.
- Excellent troubleshooting and problem solving skills.

Requirements (Desired)
- Action Script.

Recommended Certifications
C017, C103, C114

J164 Senior EJB Programmer

Description
- Define, design, and code complex, multi-tier distributed software applications.
- Develop and execute unit tests. In addition, provide technical guidance to QA in test strategy and test case development.
- Collaborate with technical writers to create installation and operations documentation.

Requirements
- Solid Java development experience.
- Experience in design and coding with EJB.
- Experience in building applications using J2EE (JMS, EJB, JSP and JDBC) and SQL modeling.
- Experience with XML, XML Schema, SOAP XDoclet, Ant and Linux.
- Experience in object-oriented design methodology.
- Able to independently design, code and test major features, as well as work jointly with other team members.
- Strong written and verbal communication skills.

Recommended Certifications
C017, C056, C100, C101, C102, C114, C150

J165 Scientific Programmer

Description
- Participate in the creation of new algorithms and proving these concepts based on field data.
- Verify the robustness of algorithms in realistic environments and to improve their performance.

Requirements
- BSc or MSc in Electrical Engineering, Physics, Applied Mathematics, Computer Science with Science and Mathematics background and experience.
- Knowledge of signal processing techniques, programming with MATLAB, C++, and FORTRAN.
- Good and broad technical background.
- Interested in expanding technical skills and applications.
- Working both independently and in a team environment.

Requirements (Desired)
- Familiarity with Linux and UNIX operation systems.

Recommended Certifications
C017

J166 Software Engineer-Programmer

Description
- Design, develop and write ATE software to perform automated tests on the Company's products.
- Assist in supporting all software needs and interfaces for the Company's products.
- Involve original design and software engineering, as well as debugging and maintenance of existing software.
- Software upgrade, interpreting specifications, perform troubleshooting, debug and maintain ATE programs, write and/or assist in writing user manuals.

Requirements
- BSc in Electrical Engineering or equivalent.
- Experience with C, Visual C++ and Visual Basic.
- Ability to program applications and an understanding of developing software to directly access hardware interfaces.
- Experience with DSP, Analog and Digital design, and RF.
- Knowledge and experience with IEEE488 interface specifications in both hardware and software.

Requirements (Desired)
- Familiar with EEPROM technology.

Recommended Certifications
C108, C116, C122

J167 Web Database Programmer

Description
- Integrate Crystal Reports and Excel to Web SQL database.

Requirements
- Programmer and Web development experience.
- Database administrator experience.
- Experience with Java, SQL, DBA and Crystal reports.

Recommended Certifications
C100, C102, C108, C110, C113, C116, C117, C119, C122, C138, C150

J168 Web CGI Programmer

Description
- Develop CGI Programming for CGI Engines.

Requirements
- Programmer analyst experience.
- Web developer experience.
- Experience with CGI Scripting, UNIX, SQL, MySQL, Token Ring and Perl Scripting.

Recommended Certifications
C108, C114, C116, C117, C119, C122

J169 Web Site Optimizer/Programmer

Description
- Optimize websites (given training).
- Check all requirements are met and thoroughly.
- Check and test the websites before published online.

Requirements
- Experience in ASP and ability to produce HTML code manually.
- Good knowledge about HTML, CSS.
- Experience of working in a team of programmers.

Requirements (Desired)
- Knowledge about PHP, JavaScript, DHTML.
- Copywriting, Client facing experience and Web site Optimization.

Recommended Certifications
C103, C107, C119

J170 Windows Game Programmer

Description
- Able to play well with others' in the development team and in the rest of the company.

- Response for the full life-cycle of projects, including requirements design, technical design, task estimation, implementation, automated testing, debugging, and deployment.

Requirements

- BSc (or higher) in Computer Science.
- Experience professional software development.
- Experience C++ development.
- Experience with localized and cross-platform product development.
- Strong understanding of end-user experience.
- Experience with DirectX and OpenGL.
- Facility with object-oriented design and implementation.

Requirements (Desired)

- Experience implementing and deploying video games.
- Experience developing/deploying networked multiplayer games.
- Familiarity with relational databases.

Recommended Certifications

C114

CHAPTER

11 COMPUTER SECURITY JOBS

Computer Security refers to techniques for ensuring that data stored in a computer cannot be read or compromised by unauthorized people. Computer security is the prevention of, or protection against:

- Access to information by unauthorized recipients.
- Intentional but unauthorized destruction or alteration of that information1.

Security is the ability of a system to protect information and system resources with respect to confidentiality and integrity.

J171 Head of IT Security/IT Security Technical Architect

Description
- Responsible for IT technical security and strategy definition.
- Define and produce security technology roadmaps and security design and delivery for multi projects.

Requirements
- Experience of security technologies and infrastructure.
- Excellent interpersonal and communication skills.

Recommended Certifications
C020

J172 Information Security Analyst

Description
- Play a key role within global enterprise monitoring, maintaining and improving the company's security architecture.
- Remain at the cutting edge of security issues surrounding network and data security as well as strike the right balance between the need to protect data and systems and the need to run the business with a high level of customer satisfaction.
- Write and implement security policies, standards and guidelines.
- Research new technologies from a security viewpoint and assist all staff in the implementation of day-to-day security measures.

Requirements
- Professional experience in an IT-related role.
- Experience working in an information security role.

Recommended Certifications
C001, C005, C020

J173 Information Security Consultant

Description
- Play a critical function to the stability and integrity of an organization framework.

Requirements

- Certification in CLAS, CHECK, CISSP etc.
- Technical background in security, systems administration and development.
- Experience with Vulnerability Assessments-Network, Penetration Testing-Network, Host, Enterprise IDS and Operating System.
- Experience with LAN, WAN, MAN, AP, SMTP, FTP, Frame Relay, ATM, FDDI, DSL, ISDN, PKI, LDAP, Identity Management, Directories, Access Management and Wireless Communication technologies (WiFi, Microwave, Bluetooth and Satellite).
- Experience with Malicious software control and countermeasures, Security Audit, UNIX Security and NT/Windows security.

- Experience with Firewall and router configuration, switches, secure network architecture, Ethernet Token Ring. As well as Hardware and Software Encryption techniques and technologies.

Recommended Certifications

C003, C004, C006, C007, C009, C020, C098, C099, C121

J174 Internet Security Tester

Description

- Perform remote penetration tests.
- Install, troubleshoot, support of Firewall products and on-site work.

Requirements

- Understanding of TCP/IP Networking and Internet security.
- Familiar with Windows and knowledge of Linux or Unix Basic.
- Understanding of routers and have product knowledge on: Checkpoint Firewall, MAILsweeper and WebSweeper.

Recommended Certifications

C001, C017, C018, C020, C021

J175 IP Security Engineer

Description

- Design and implement secure networks.
- Design end to end network security solutions; implement a defense strategy, and managing network security.

Requirements

- Security Engineer experience.
- Experience with IP protocols, VPN, IPSEC, OS (Linux, BSD, HP-UX and Solaris), IDS and pen testing. As well as checkpoint firewall skills with exposure to either Watchguard or Netscreen.

Recommended Certifications

C006, C007, C009, C017, C020

J176 IT Security Manager

Description

- Information Security Managers on their behalf will work as well as Consultants to be based on one of their key client sites which feature in the Banking/financial services sector.
- This role will give security experts the opportunity to work with cutting-edge technology within a consultancy that is further ahead in the security field than its competitors.
- Responsible for delivering Information Security Management solutions.

Requirements
- Security professionals experience of delivering Information Security solutions in OS Windows.
- Experience with Active Directory, VPN, Smart Cards, Vulnerability Management, Enterprise-Wide User Administration, Mainframes and Security Performance Measurement.

Recommended Certifications
C020, C098

J177 Network Security Analyst

Description
- Support and maintain a number of Firewalls.
- Provide resolutions for any service outage or user problem.

Requirements
- Experience of Network Security across several platforms, concentrating on Cisco Pix Firewall installation/configuration, Cisco Routers and Switch access control lists.
- Knowledge of Nokia, Checkpoint, Boardware, Cyberguard firewall configuration, Network Address Translation, Port Address Translation and Mail, Web Marshal.

Recommended Certifications
C009, C018, C020

J178 Network Security Engineer

Description
- Responsible for network analysis, support, projects work, security analysis, security reporting, security implementations and security project work.

Requirements
- Background of financial (trading, investment bank and production environment), Arrowpoint, PIX, Checkpoint firewalls, Intrusion Detection Systems, Network Management Tools and Bandwidth Analysis.
- Experience running CISCO networks (routers and switches, LAN and WAN) with excellent security skills and knowledge.
- UNIX administration and Perl scripting skills.

Recommended Certifications
C003, C004, C005, C006, C007, C009, C017, C018, C020

J179 SAP Security & Authorizations Consultant

Description
- Participate in international project rollout efforts, systems support and optimization.

Requirements
- Experience with R/3 Security issues, role/profile development, Profile Generator etc.
- Experience of Security Audits and Testing, and BW Authorizations.

Recommended Certifications
C020

J180 Security Analysts

Description
- Work on projects of varying complexity for a global IT consultancy.
- Low-level design and implementation of security subsystems (firewalls, VPN, IDS and AV subsystems).

Requirements
- Cisco accredited (CCNA, CCNP or higher).
- Experience of implementing security subsystems, secure network design and implementation.
- Ability to justify requirements for secure network architecture to colleagues and clients alike.
- Experience in team leading roles and able to be security cleared.

Requirements (Desired)
- Penetration testing experience.

Recommended Certifications
C005, C006, C007, C009, C020

J181 Security Designer

Description
- Develop and implement high end Security solutions.

Requirements
- Experience in the design of infrastructure security solutions.
- Knowledge of secure design principles as well as the components of security architectures, key protocols, internetworking standards, web applications, network topologies and common infrastructure.
- Technical expertise and excellent people management skills.

Recommended Certifications
C009, C020

J182 Security Technical Architect

Description
- Responsible for overall IT technical security.
- Deliver a technical infrastructure roadmap to meet known current/future technical and commercial requirements and evolve this as these changes.

- Work with IT colleagues and external suppliers to ensure that appropriate technology direction is set and investments are made which best support the commercial requirements of the company.
- Work with the BATAS and BAPMS, the other Technical Architects, the CTO and other colleagues to anticipate and understand the forward demand from the business areas.
- Work with other architectural colleagues to develop a service based architecture and roadmap which will enable a more rapid and cost effective delivery of business solutions.
- Work with other architectural colleagues to shape, define and agree the overall corporate technology strategy.
- Gain agreement at all levels up-to and including Board level. Also define and commission the projects that will implement the strategy and ensure that funding is secured.
- Work with the project managers to ensure the successful delivery of the projects. In addition own the technical responsibility for the introduction of new technologies.
- Work with commercial and IT colleagues to shape and develop IT solution options, IT resource options and IT delivery plans that meet commercial requirements.
- Maintain an up-to-date knowledge of industry trends and emerging standards.
- Conform to a defined architecture and systems delivery method.
- Drive innovative use of technology for the benefit of the company.

Requirements
- Experience in IT security and senior architectural role.
- Experience in delivery of architecture security for large complex projects and security design.
- Experience of anticipating technology and business needs as opposed to reacting to immediate demands or events.
- Experience in defining strategy and in production of security technology roadmaps such as for User authentication, systems and network access, messaging based application security.
- Experience of strategic decision making leading to investments.

Recommended Certifications
C006, C007, C009, C020

J183 Security Team Manager

Description
- Responsible for planning, directing and coordinating the integration of security requirements and solutions into business programs to ensure the integrity of the network, systems and services provided to customers and to protect the business.
- Develop and coordinate specialist technical expertise to influence decision-making critical to business programs and establish the company as a leader in security technology.

Requirements
- Experience of Project Management.

- Experience in developing and managing highly motivated teams of security champions across either Network Security, IS Security or Internet Security.

Requirements (Desired)
- CISSP.

Recommended Certifications
C009, C019, C020, C098

J184 Security Test Engineer

Description
- Provide technical and business recommendations on product development issues.

Requirements
- Security experience and a thorough knowledge of SSL, IPSec, PKI, encryption and/or cryptography.
- Formal testing experience, gained testing relevant security or network centric products.
- Any hands on development using Java and/or C#.
- Experience of a software/product development company.

Recommended Certifications
C009, C020, C100, C102, C122

J185 Senior Lead Designer Security

Description
- Develop and implement practical, flexible designs that are aligned to technical roadmaps.
- Involve project management with different business streams also have Technical Management of junior lead designers and provide advice and support in the creation of practical design solutions.
- Drive the development of new design in the technical stream area and have a strong appreciation of how the interfaces into other technical areas.

Requirements
- Experience in the design of infrastructure security solutions and have a strong awareness of Industry trends in IT security, different standards/processes.
- Experience in application security, knowledge of secure design principles as well as the components of security architectures.
- Knowledge of key protocols and internetworking standards, web applications in a Microsoft environment, windows networking and platforms, network topologies and communications infrastructure, remote access technologies.
- Great team skills and excellent people management skills.

Recommended Certifications
C003, C004, C009, C018, C019, C020, C108, C119

J186 Senior Professional Services Security Consultant

Description
- Involve delivery of workshops, architecture and deployment planning, presenting to clients, project management, pre-sales.
- Work on responses to RFI/P and mentoring other consultants.

Requirements
- Good technical degree and must have in-depth knowledge in one or more of the following technology areas: Web Access Management, Web based Single Sign-on, Identity Management, Authentication Technologies (tokens, X.509, SMS), Internet Security Architectures, Security Toolkits, Application Servers, Portals and PKI.
- Have a consultancy background with experience in bidding for solutions, projects management, integration projects, appreciation of software engineering practices and procedures, and Web Based technologies.

Recommended Certifications
C009, C019, C020, C021, C098, C099, C108, C115, C122

J187 Senior Security Consultant

Description
- Produce technical security policies.
- Liaise with both the business users in a more conceptual capacity as well as being able to go in-depth with technical experts.
- Write security policies and standards.
- Provide an excellent learning curve and cutting edge security work.

Requirements
- Master in Information Security or CISSP).
- Technical knowledge in BS/ISO, security architecture methodologies, strong networking knowledge, encryption and cryptography and a strong grounding in OS Security issues.

Recommended Certifications
C009, C020, C098

J188 Senior Security Management Consultant

Description
- Provide leadership to teams involved in the implementation of security services and related projects, therefore the oversight of corresponding technologies and processes eg PKI, SMS and validation services etc.
- Responsible for evaluating the clients' business strategy, objectives and requirements.
- Using advanced consulting methodologies, translate the clients long range business plan into a services strategy.

- Build trust with the customer and establish his needs and how the client can help, lead the sales of consulting services, lead the delivery of consulting services, develop solutions.
- Write accurate and effective statements of work, identify and pursue new business opportunities, conceptualize architects, designs, implement and support integrated solutions.
- Able to interface at CIO, CSO, COO and CEO level executives.

Requirements
- Extensive security infrastructure experience.
- Experience of winning assignments and delivering them via formal bid processes and consultative selling.

Recommended Certifications
C009, C014, C020

J189 Senior Technical Security Architect

Description
- Responsible for gathering requirements and looking at the external regulatory requirements and the product agnostics.
- Design the security solutions on a number of projects and looking at the solution from a technical point of view.

Requirements
- Systems Integrator Experience.
- Security Architect and Security Designer experience.
- Experience with Firewalls, Anti-Virus, Networking and Security.

Recommended Certifications
C005, C006, C007, C009, C018, C020

J190 Technical Security Specialist

Description
- Provide support to Technical Security and client customers through security risk assessments and recommendation of appropriate security solutions.
- Respond to security requests and approvals.
- Maintain supplier relationships and promotes the use of new technologies, standards and plans to ensure the integrity of the network, systems and services provided to customers and to protect the business.

Requirements
- Strong knowledge of security aspects.
- Experience with OS environments, GSM, GPRS and 3G experience through design or deployment.
- People management and process development skills.

Recommended Certifications
C009, C019, C20, C021

GLOSSARY

.msi	File Extensions: Installer package (Microsoft Windows)
.Net	Dot NET
3Com	Computers, Communication and Compatibility
4GL	Fourth-Generation Languages
A+	The A+ certification demonstrates competency as a computer technician
Active X	Set of platform independent technologies developed by Microsoft that enable software components to interact with one another in a networked environment, like the Internet
adhoc	Meaning "to this" in Latin, it refers to dealing with special situations as they occur rather than functions that are repeated on a regular basis
ADO.NET	ActiveX Data Objects
ads	Advertisements
AICC	Aviation Industry Computer-Based Training Committee
AIX	Athens Internet Exchange
AJAX	Asynchronous JAvaScript and XML
Ant	Another Neat Tool
AOC	Administrative Operations Committee
Apache	A web server for Unix-like systems, Microsoft Windows, Novell NetWare and other operating systems. Apache is notable for playing a key role in the initial growth of the World Wide Web
APC	Automatic Ping Control
API	Application Programming Interface
App	Application
ARCH	Designing Cisco Network Architectures
AS/400	Application System/400
ASA	Active Server Application or Adaptive Security Algorithm or Adaptive Server Anywhere
ASE	Adaptive Server Enterprise - A relational DBMS from Sybase that runs on Windows NT/2000, Linux and a variety of Unix platforms
ASM	Association for Systems Management
ASP	Active Server Page
ASP.Net	ASP dot Net
ASPX	.NET Active Server Page
ATE	Automatic Test Equipment
ATEC	Microsoft Authorized Academic Training Program
ATG	Art Technology Group
ATS	Advanced Technical Specialists

Avaya IP Office	An intelligent communications solution specially designed to meet the communications challenges facing small and midsized businesses
AWK	Alfred Aho, Peter Weinberger, Brian Kernighan
B2B	Business-To-Business
BA	Bachelor of arts
BASH	Bourne Again SHell shell
BCMSN	Building Cisco Multilayer Switched Networks
BCRAN	Building Cisco Remote Access Networks
BEA	Basic programming Environment
BGP	Border Gateway Protocol
BI	Business Intelligence
BICSI	Building Scalable Cisco Internet-works
BIND	Berkeley Internet Name Daemon
Biztalk	Microsoft's logo for business-to-business and application-to-application integration
Bloomberg	Applications Program Interface (API) allows you to download the broad variety of global market data directly from Bloomberg into Excel
BREW	Binary Runtime Environment for Wireless
Brocade	A company producing storage systems
BSAE	Bachelor of Science Architectural Engineering
Bsc	Bachelor of Science
BSCI	Building Scalable Cisco Internet-works
BSD	Berkeley Software Distribution
BSME	Bachelor of Science in Mechanical Engineering
BSS	Billing Systems
BUD	Business User Development
C	C Language
C#	C-sharp
C++	C-plus plus
CA	Computer Associates
CAN	Certified Novell Administrator
CAPM™	Certified Associate in Project Management
CATIA	Computer Aided Three dimensional Interactive Application
CBK	Common Body of Knowledge
CCDA	Cisco Certified Design Associate
CCDP	Cisco Certified Design Professional
CCI	Citrix Certified Instructor
CCIE	Cisco Certified Internet-work Expert
CCIP	Cisco Certified Internet-work Professional
CCNA	CISCO Certified Network Associate
CCNA	Cisco Certified Network Administrator

CCNP	Cisco Certified Network Professional
CCNS	Cisco Content Networking Specialist
CCR	Certification Requirements Program
CCRs	Continuing Certification Requirements
CCSI	Certified Cisco Systems Instructor
CCSP	Cisco Certified Security Professional
CCTV	Closed Circuit Television
CDE	Certified Directory Engineer
CDIA+	Certified Document Imaging Architects
CDMA	Code Division Multiple Access
CDROM	Compact Disk Read Only Memory
CE	Computer Engineering
CentOS	Community ENTerprise Operating System
CGI	Common Gateway Interface
CICS	Customer Information Control System
Cisco	A leading supplier of communications and computer networking products, systems, and services
CISSP	Certified Information Systems Security Professional
CIT	Cisco Internet-work Troubleshooting Support
Citrix	The leader in access infrastructure solutions, which includes network access, single sign-on, VPN capabilities, presentation services, remote control and remote support applications
CIW	Certified Internet Webmaster
CLE	Certified Linux Engineer
ClearCase	A software configuration management (SCM) system for client/server environments from IBM
CLP	Certified Linux Professional
CLR	Common Language Runtime
CMS	Content Management Systems
CNE	Certified Novell Engineer
CNI	Certified Novell Instructor
Cognos	Cognos knows that smart business requires intelligence
ColdFusion	An application development tool from Macromedia for writing Web pages that interact with databases
COM	Component Object Model
COM+	An extension of COM
CommVault	A United States based company specializing in data and storage management software
Compaq	Compaq Computer Corporation
CompTIA	Computing Technology Industry Association
CompuMentor	One of the leading providers of technology assistance to non-profit organizations in the United States

COP	Cisco Optical Specialist
Corba	Common Object Request Broker Architecture
CPAN	Comprehensive Perl Archive Network
cPanel	Control Panel
CPC	Collaborative Product Commerce
CPE	Continuing Professional Education
CPM	Corporate Performance Management
CPSR	Contractor Purchasing System Review
CPU	Central Processing Unit
CRM	Customer Relationship Management
Santa Cruz Operations	SCO Group, a leading vendor of Unix operating systems for the x86 platform
CS	Computer Science
CSS	Cascading Style Sheets
CTECs	Microsoft Certified Technical Education Centers
CTO	Chief Technical Officer
CTT+	Certified Technical Trainer
Cut	Control Unit Terminal
CV	Curriculum Vitae
CVS	Concurrent Versioning System - an open-source version control system
DataStage	A data extraction and transformation program for Windows NT/2000 servers that is used to pull data from legacy databases
DB	Database
DB2	IBM's flagship relational database management system
DBA	Database Administrator
DBD	DataBase Driver
DBI	DataBase Interface
DCN	Designing Cisco Networks
DCOM	Distributed Component Object Model
DealMaven	Provides financial analysis and modeling training resources, as well as productivity enhancing software tools for Microsoft Office
Debian	A project based around the development of a free, complete operating system
Dell	A leading PC manufacturer, founded in 1984 by Michael Dell
DHCP	Dynamic Host Configuration Protocol
DHTML	Dynamic Hyper Text Markup Language
DirXML	The code name for directory interchange software from Novell that integrates NDS with other directories in Exchange, Lotus Notes, Windows 2000 (Active Directory) and others.
DMZ	De-Militarised Zone
DNS	Domain Name System
DOM	Document Object Model

DOS	Disk Operating System - A single-user operating system from Microsoft for the PC
Dreamweaver	A Web authoring program for Windows and the Macintosh from Macromedia
DSL	Digital Subscriber Line
DSP	Digital Signal Processing
DTS	Data Transfer Service
DVD	Digital VideoDisc
DW	Data Warehouse
DWDM	Dense Wave Division Multiplexing
EAP	Extensible Authentication Protocol
eBay	The major auction service on the Web
e-Biz+	E-Business concepts and technologies
E-Commerce	Electronic Commerce
EDI	Electronic Data Interchange
eDirectory	A hierarchical, object oriented database that represents all the assets in an organization in a logical tree
EE	Electronic Engineering
EEPROM	Electrically Erasable Programmable Read Only Memory
EGL	Enterprise Generation Language
EJB	Extend Java Beans
EJBTM	Extend JavaBeansTM
E-Mail	Electronic mail
EMC	The leading supplier of storage products for midrange computers and mainframes
EOE	Execution Only Environment
ERP	Enterprise Resource Planning
ETL	Extract, Transform, Load
Exchange Server	An Internet-compliant messaging system that runs under Windows NT/2000
FACSys	The first LAN Fax platform for Windows NT
Factset	FactSet Research Systems
FCIP	Fibre Channel over IP - A protocol for tunneling Fibre Channel data across an IP network
FDA	Financial Divorce Association
Fireworks	Known as FW for short, is a bitmap and vector graphics editor
Flash	A multimedia authoring and playback system from Adobe
FortiNet	Is a private company, that specializes in network security appliances
FORTRAN	FORmula TRANslator
FreeBSD	Unix-like free operating system, Berkeley Software Distribution (BSD)
FrontPage	A popular Web authoring program from Microsoft for Windows and the Mac

FTP	File Transfer Protocol
FTSS	Field Technical Sales Support
Fusebox	A popular web development framework for ColdFusion and other web development languages
Geophysics	Branch of Geology, Physics, Science
GFS	Global File System
GIF	Graphics Interchange Format
Go/No-Go	Is a process or device used in quality control
Goldmine	Is a Customer Relationship Management software package
GPA	Grade Point Average
GPO	Group Policy Object
Groupwise	Messaging and groupware software from Novell that provides a universal inbox for calendaring, group scheduling, task management, document sharing, workflow and threaded discussions
GSA	General Services Administration
GSM	Global System for Mobile communication
GUI	Graphical User Interface
HCI	Human Computer Interaction
H/W	Hardware
HFi	Human Factors Integration
Hibernate	A Java-based object-relational mapping/persistence framework
HIPAA	Health Insurance Portability and Accountability Act
Hitwise	Is an internet monitor which collects data directly from ISP networks
HL7	Health Level 7
HP	Hewlett-Packard,
HPCT	High Performance Computing Technology
HPS	Securing Hosts Using Cisco Security Agent
HP-UX	Hewlett-Packard's version of Unix
HR	Human Resources
HTI	Home Technology Integrator
HTML	Hyper Text Markup Language
HTTP	Hyper-Text Transport Protocol
HTTPS	HyperText Transfer Protocol Secure
IBM	International Business Machines Corporation
IBMers	IBM employees
ICND	Interconnecting Cisco Network Devices
ICP	Instructor Certification Process
IDDQ	Is a method for testing CMOS integrated circuits for the presence of manufacturing faults
IDIQ	Indefinite Delivery Indefinite Quantity
IDS	Intrusion Detection System

IEEE	Institute of Electrical and Electronics Engineers
IEEE488	IEEE Standard Digital Interface for Programmable Instrumentation
iFCP	Internet Fibre Channel Protocol
IGRP	Interior Gateway Routing Protocol
IIS	Internet Information Services
ImageReady	Is a bitmap graphics editor shipped with Adobe Photoshop by Adobe Systems
IMAP	Internet Message Access Protocol
iMode	Japanese network NTT DoCoMo
IMS	Information Management System
InDesign	A desktop publishing (DTP) application produced by Adobe Systems
i-Net+	Internet, intranet, extranet skills
Informix	A relational database management system (DBMS) from IBM that runs on a variety of Unix platforms
Interwoven	The leading provider of Enterprise Content Management (ECM) solutions that empower enterprises
INTRO	Introduction to Cisco Networking Technologies
IOS	Internetwork Operating System
IP	Internet Protocol
Iplanet	The brand name for software from the Sun-Netscape Alliance
IP-PBX	Internet Protocol Private Branch eXchange
IPS	Implementing Cisco Intrusion Prevention System
IP-SEC	IP SECurity
IPX	Internetwork Packet Exchange - The network layer protocol in the NetWare operating system
IQA	Institute of Quality Assurance
IR	Information Retrieval
Irix	Unix-based operating system from SGI
IronPort	Is an email and web security products provider for network management and protection against Internet threats
IS	Information Systems
I-SA	IBM Certified Infrastructure Systems Architect
ISAPI	Internet Server Application Programming Interface
ISC2	International Information Systems Security Certification Consortium ((ISC)2)
iSCSI	Internet SCSI) A protocol that serializes SCSI commands and converts them to TCP/IP
iSeries	A family of midrange servers from IBM that are based on IBM's POWER CPUs and run under the i5/OS, OS/400 and AIX operating systems
ISO	International Organization for Standardization
ISP	Internet Service Provider - Information Systems Professional
ISS	Information System Security

IT	Information Technology
ITIL	Information Technology Infrastructure Library
IVR	Interactive Voice Response
J2EE	Java 2 Enterprise Edition
J2EETM	Java 2 Enterprise EditionTM
J2ME	Java2 Micro Edition
Java	An object-oriented programming language developed by Sun Microsystems
JavaBeans	A component software architecture from Sun that runs in the Java environment
JavaScript	A popular scripting language that is widely supported in Web browsers and other Web tools
JBoss	Jay Boss - an Open Source J2EE-based application server implemented in Java
jCED	jCert Enterprise Developer
jCert	Java Technology Certification
jCJP	jCert Java Programmer
JCL	Java Class Library
jCSD	jCert Solution Developer
JDBC	Java Database Connectivity
JDBCTM	A JavaTM API for executing SQL statements
Jini	A Java-based distributed computing environment from Sun
JMF	Java Media Framework
JMS	Java Messenging Service
JNDI	Java Naming and Directory Interface
JPG	Joint Photographers Graphic
JSP	Java Server Page
JSPTM	JavaServer PagesTM
JSR	Java Portlet Specification
JSTL	JavaServer Pages Standard Tag Library
JUnit	Unit test framework for the Java programming language
LAMP	Linux, Apache, MySQL, P for PHP, Perl and Python - The core set of applications and languages used in a Linux Web server
LAN	Local Area Network
Lava	An experimental, object-oriented, interpreter-based programming language with an associated programming environment
Lawson	A software company that specializes in enterprise resource planning (ERP)
LCIP	Local Community Interest Programming
LDAP	Lightweight Directory Access Protocol
Legato	A leading provider of storage management and high-availability software founded in 1988
LID	Light-Weight Identity
Lingo	A scripting language developed by John H

Linux	Linus Torvald's UNIX - A very popular version of the Unix operating system that runs on a variety of hardware platforms
LiveVault	The leading provider of fully managed offsite backup, online backup and recovery services
Log4j	A Java-based logging utility
Lotus	A major software company founded in 1981 by Mitch Kapor
LPAR	Logical PARtition - A logical segmentation of a mainframe's memory and other resources
LTX	An Automatic Test Equipment (ATE) vendor, founded in 1976
Mac	Macintosh
MAC OS	MACintosh Operating System
Mac OSX	The current operating system from Apple for the Macintosh family
Macromedia	A software company specializing in multimedia authoring tools that was acquired by Adobe Systems
Malware	MALicious softWARE - Software designed to destroy, aggravate and otherwise make life unhappy
Marimba	A software company founded in 1996 by four key members of Sun's original Java development team
MATLAB	MATrix LABoratory - A programming language for technical computing from The MathWorks
MBA	Master of Business Administration
MBIST	Memory BIST (Built-in Self Test)
MBS	Microsoft Business Solution certification
MCAD	Microsoft Certified Application Developer
MCAP	Microsoft Certified Architect Program
McData	A corporation that provides storage area networking (SAN) products and services
MCDBA	Microsoft Certified Database Administrator
MCDST	Microsoft Certified Desktop Support Technician
MCITP	Microsoft Certified IT Professional
MCLC	Microsoft Certified Learning Consultant
MCNE	Master Certified Novell Engineer
MCNI	Master Certified Novell Instructor
MCP	Microsoft Certified Professional
MCPD	Microsoft Certified Professional Developer
MCSA	Microsoft Certified Systems Administrator
MCSD	Microsoft Certified Solution Developer
MCSE	Microsoft Certified Systems Engineer
MCT	Microsoft Certified Trainer
MCTS	Microsoft Certified Technology Specialist
MCTs	Microsoft Certified Trainers
MDX	Multidimensional Expressions

MFC	Microsoft Foundation Class - An application framework for writing Microsoft C/C++ and Visual C++ applications
Microsoft	The most successful and influential software company
Microstrategy	A business intelligence, Enterprise Reporting, and OLAP software vendor
middleware	Software that functions as a conversion or translation layer
MIME	Multipurpose Internet Mail Extensions
MIT	Massachusetts Institute of Technology
MMS	Multimedia Message Service
mock-ups	Are used by designers mainly to acquire feedback from users about designs and design ideas early in the design process
Mod_Perl	Software that integrates Perl programming with the Apache Web server
Modernbill	Billing Software is the most advanced automated and recurring billing solution on the market today
MOS	Microsoft Office Specialist
MPLS	MultiProtocol Label Switching - A standard from the IETF for including routing information in the packets of an IP network
MQ	Message Queue
MQ Series	Messaging middleware from IBM that allows programs to communicate with each other across all IBM platforms
MRB	Mineral Resources Branch
MS	MicroSoft
MS SQL	Microsoft SQL Server
Msc	Master of Science
MSF	Microsoft Solutions Framework
MSI	MicroSoft Installer
MSMQ	Microsoft Message Queue Server
MSP's	Management Service Provider
MVC	Model-View-Controller
MVC/Struts	A framework for writing Web-based applications in Java that supports the MVC architecture
MVS	Multiple Virtual Storage
MX	An edition
MyNetonomy	Suite of customer self-service applications allows consumers and business customers to activate and manage subscriptions
MySQL	A very popular open source, relational DBMS from MySQL AB, Uppsala, Sweden
NAS	Network Attached Storage
NBX	Network Branch Exchange - A family of IP-based telephony systems from 3Com
NDMP	Network Data Management Protocol - An open standard for backing up data in a heterogeneous environment
NEON	Nevada Education Online Network
NetApp	Network Appliance, Inc

NetGenesis	Web analytics solutions transform high volumes of Web data into actionable e-metrics, measurements of e-business success
NFS	Network File System
NIC	Network Interface Card
NIS	Network Information Service
NNTP	Network News Transfer Protocol
Novell	A firm believer in the power of networking
NS	Novell Specialist
NT	Windows NT
OCA	Oracle Database Administrator Certified Associate
OCM	Oracle Database Administrator Certified Master
OCP	Oracle Database Administrator Certified Professional
OCP	Oracle Internet Applications Develop Rel. 6ir Certified Professional
ODA	Official Development Assistance
ODBC	Open DataBase Connectivity
CLI	Call Level Interface - A database programming interface from the SQL Access Group (SAG)
OEM	Original Equipment Manufacturer - a company that assembles complete pieces of equipment from parts
OJT	On-the-Job Training
OLTP	OnLine Transaction Processing
OnDemand iSeries	part of the IBM Content Manager portfolio for enterprise content management
Onyx	A stack based programming language with many powerful features
OO	Object Oriented
OOAD	Object Oriented Analysis and Design
OOD	Object-Oriented Design
OOM	Object-Oriented Modeling
OOP	Object Oriented Programming
OpenGL	OPEN Graphics Language - a 3D graphics language developed by SGI
Oracle	Oak Ridge Automatic Computer and Logical Engine
OS	Operating System
OS/2	A family of multitasking operating systems for x86 machines from IBM
OS/390	The primary operating system used in IBM mainframes
OSPF	Open Shortest Path First
OSS	Operational Systems
OSX	Operating System from Apple
Pc	Personal Computer
PCD	Planned Commercial and Office District
PDA	Personal Data Assistance
PDF	Portable Document Format

PDLC	Product Data Life Cycle
PDM	Portal Document Manager
PDUs	Professional Development Units
PeopleSoft	A software company that specializes in enterprise-wide applications for client/server environments
Percussion	Software provides an enterprise-ready Web Content Management System (WCM)
Perl	Practical Extraction Report Language
Ph.D	Doctorate Degree
Photoshop	A popular high-end image editor for the Macintosh and Windows from Adobe
PHP	Hypertext Preprocessor
PIOS	Production Inventory Optimization System
PIX	family of network firewalls from Cisco
PKI	Public Key Infrastructure
PL/SQL	Procedural Language/Structured Query Language
Plumtree	A software company headquartered in San Francisco, California. Founded in 1996, Plumtree pioneered the development of corporate portal software
PMBOK	Project Management Body of Knowledge
PMBOK®	Project Management Body of Knowledge
PMI	The Project Management Institute
PMI®	Project Management Institute
PMPs	Project Management Professionals
POOM	Pocket Outlook Object Model
POP3	Post Office Protocol
portlet	A small window on a portal page
POS	Packet Over SONET (Synchronous Optical NETwork)
PostgreSQL	A free software object-relational database management system (ORDBMS)
PPC	Pay per click, a method of charging for advertising on the Internet
PPTP	Point-to-Point Tunneling Protocol
Proxy	A computer system or router that breaks the connection between sender and receiver
PSO	Product Support Officer
PTT	Push-to-Talk
PXE	Preboot EXecution Environment
Python	A popular, object-oriented scripting language used for writing system utilities and Internet scripts
QA	Qality Assurance
Qmail	Mail transfer agent that runs on Unix
QoS	Quality of Service
RAC	Real Application Clusters
RAD	Rational Application Developer

RAID	Redundant Array of Independent Disks
RCS	Revision Control System
RDBMS	Relational Database Management System
RedHat	A software company founded in 1994 by Marc Ewing and Bob Young that specializes in distributing the open source Linux operating system
Rel.	An Open Source true relational database management system (TRDBMS)
RF	Radio Frequency
RHCA	RedHat Certified Architect
RHCE	RedHat Certified Engineer
RHCT	RedHat Certified Technician
RHEL	Linux RedHat Enterprise
Rhythmyx	An enterprise-strength Web Content Management System for multi-channel, customer-centric applications
RIP	Routing Information Protocol
RMI	Remote Method Invocation
ROI	Return On Investment - The monetary benefits derived from having spent money on developing or revising a system
RPG	Report Program Generator - One of the first program generators designed for business reports, introduced in 1964 by IBM
ILE	Integrated Language Environment - enables C, Java and other modules to be integrated into the program
Ruby	An interpreted, object-oriented programming language that is somewhat similar to Perl in syntax
RUP	Rational Unified Process
S/390	Originally an abbreviation for IBM's System/390 machines
SAFE	Security and Freedom through Encryption
SAMBA	Free software that allows a Unix server to act as a file server to Windows clients
SAN	Storage Area Network
Santa Cruz Operation	A leading vendor of Unix operating systems for the x86 platform
SAP	Systems Applications Processing
SAS	Statistical Analysis System
SAX	Simple API for XML
SCAN	To read a printed form a line at a time in order to convert images into bit-mapped representations or convert characters into text
SCE	Service Creation Environments
SCORM	Sharable Content Object Reference Model
SCSI	Small Computer System Interface - a hardware interface that allows for the connection of up to 15 peripheral devices to a single PCI board
SDLC	Software Development Life Cycle
SDLS	Specification Description Language Diagrams
SED	Stream EDitor
SEI	Software Engineering Institute

Sendmail	An SMTP-based message transfer agent
SEO	Search Engine Optimization
Servlets	A Java application that runs in a Web server or application server and provides server-side processing such as accessing a database and e-commerce transactions
SH	Shell
Sharepoint	A Microsoft brand for software that enables a Web site to provide document and information sharing
shell	A piece of software that provides an interface for users (command line interpreter)
Siebel	A family of Web-based customer relationship management (CRM) applications from Siebel Systems
SIP	Session Initiation Protocol
SLAs	Service-Level Agreements
Smarty	A web template system written in PHP
SMIL	Synchronized Media Integration Language
SML	Simple Markup Language
SMS	Short Message Service
SMTP	Simple Mail Transfer Protocol
SND	Securing Cisco Network Devices
SNMP	Simple Network Management Protocol
SNPA	Securing Networks with PIX and ASA
SNRS	Securing Networks with Cisco Routers and Switches
SOA	Service Oriented Architecture
SOAP	Simple Object Access Protocol
Solaris	A multitasking, multiprocessing operating system and distributed computing environment for Sun's SPARC computers from Sun
SONET/SDH	Synchronous Optical NETwork/Synchronous Digital Hierarchy) A common reference to SONET networks worldwide
Sonicwall	A company which provides hardware devices for Internet security
SOP	Super Operator
Spring	Is GIS and remote sensing image processing system with an object-oriented data model
SQA	Scottish Qualifications Authority
SQL	Structured Query Language
SSCP	System Security Certified Practitioner
SSH	Secure Shell
SSIS	SQL Server Integration Services
SSL	Secure Sockets Layer
StorageTek	A leading provider of disk and tape storage solutions and services that was founded in 1969
Struts	A framework for writing Web-based applications in Java that supports the Model-View-Controller (MVC) architecture

SumTotal	An EOE and strongly supports diversity in the workplace
SUN	A major manufacturer of Unix-based workstations and servers
SunOS	Sun's Unix operating system. SunOS was renamed Solaris
SuSE	SuSE was originally an acronym for "Software und System Entwicklung" (Software and System Development)
SVG	Scalable Vector Graphics - A vector graphics format from the W3C for the Web that is expressed in XML
SVN	Subversion - A revision control system which allows computer software to be developed in an incremental and controlled fashion by a distributed group of programmers
Swift	Society for Worldwide Interbank Financial Telecommunication
Swing	A Java toolkit for developing graphical user interfaces (GUIs).
Swishe	Simple Web Indexing System for Humans - Enhanced. Swish-e can quickly and easily index directories of files or remote web sites and search the generated indexes.
Sybase	A software company founded in 1984 that specializes in enterprise infrastructure and integration of platforms, databases and applications
Symbian	An open standard operating system for data-enabled mobile phones (smartphones)
SyncML	Synchronization Markup Language
T&M	Time and Material
TCP	Transmission Control Protocol
TEC	Tivoli Enterprise Console
Telephia	A leading worldwide provider of business intelligence software
ThinkFree Server Edition	Provides application launchers with identical icons to the ThinkFree Desktop
TIBCO	Develops software that enables the various applications, databases, and platforms used by companies to work together
TOAD	A database administration and SQL development software application
Tomcat	A popular Java servlet container from the Apache Jakarta project.
TotalStorage	IBM System Storage - the brand name for IBM's computer storage products
TSO	Time Sharing Option - Software that provides interactive communications for IBM's MVS operating system
T-SQL	Transact-SQL - Microsoft's and Sybase's proprietary extension to the SQL language
TypePad	A blogging service from company Six Apart Ltd
UDB	Universal Database
UDDI	Universal Description Discovery and Integration
UI	User Interface
UML	Unified Modelling Language

UniData	A relational DBMS from IBM that runs on the major Unix servers and Windows NT/2000
UniVerse	A relational DBMS from IBM that runs on the major Unix servers and Windows NT/2000
Unix	UNiplexed Information and Computing System - A multiuser, multitasking operating system that is widely used as the master control program in workstations and servers
VB	Visual Basic
VB.Net	Visual Basic .NET
VBA	Visual Basic for Applications
Verilog	A hardware description language (HDL) used to model electronic systems
VHDL	VHSIC Hardware Description Language
vhost	virtual host - On the Web, a server that contains multiple Web sites
VHS	Video Home System - A half-inch, analog videocassette recorder (VCR) format
Vignette	Software - A suite of content management, portal, collaboration, document management, and records management products developed by the Vignette Corporation
Visio	A drawing and diagramming program for Windows from Microsoft
Visual C	A C and C++ development system for DOS/Windows applications from Microsoft
Visual FoxPro	An Xbase development system for Windows from Microsoft
VLAN	Virtual LAN - a logical subgroup within a local area network that is created via software rather than manually moving cables in the wiring closet.
VLDB	Very Large DataBase - An extremely large database
VoIP	Voice over Internet Protocol
VP	Virtual Prototyping
VPN	Virtual Private Network
vs.	VerSus. - In contrast with
VxWorks	A popular realtime operating system for embedded systems from Wind River
W3C	World Wide Web Consortium
WAI	Web Accessibility Initiative - an effort to improve the accessibility of the Web for people using a wide range of user agent devices
WAN	Wide Area Network
WAP	Wireless protocols
WAS	WebSphere Application Server - an IBM application server
WCDMA	Wideband Code Division Multiple Access
WCM	Web Content Management
WCS	WebSphere Commerce Suite provides a complete solution for a company's electronic commerce needs
Web	The World Wide Web

Weblog software	A category of software which consists of a specialized form of Content Management Systems
Weblogic	A software suite from BEA Systems
WebMethods	WEBM, which was founded in 1996, is a company that provides business integration software
WebObjects	A sophisticated development environment from Apple for creating Web applications that run on NT, Solaris, HP/UX and OPENSTEP Mach. WebObjects enables development in Java and a variety of C versions including Objective-C and C++.
Websidestory	Founded in 1996, markets web analytics services
WebSphere	A family of Java development and Web application server products from IBM
Wiki	A Web site that can be quickly edited by its visitors with simple formatting rules
WIN	A short name for Windows; for example, Win95 or Win98
WIN2K	Windows 2000
WML	Wireless Markup Language - A tag-based language used in the Wireless Application Protocol (WAP)
WMQI	WebSphere M Q Integrator
WORM	Write-one, read-many - Pertaining to a storage device
WSAD	WebSphere Studio Application Developer
WSAD IDE	WebSphere Studio Application Developer IDE
WSDL	Web Services Description Language
WSRP	Web Services for Remote Portlets
WYSIWYG	What You See Is What You Get
XDoclet	An open-source code generation library which enables Attribute-Oriented Programming for Java via insertion of special Javadoc tags
XHTML	eXtensible HyperText Markup Language
XML	Extensible Markup Language
XO	Stationary operating
XP	eXtreme Programming
Xpath	XML PATH - A sublanguage in an XSL style sheet that is used to identify XML elements for processing
XSD	XML Schema Definition
XSL	eXtensible Style Language
XSLT	eXtensible Stylesheet Language Transformation
YP/NIS	Yellow Pages/Network Information Services - A naming service from Sun-Soft that allows resources to be easily added, deleted or relocated
z/OS	A mission critical mainframe operating system that extends OS/390 to IBM's zSeries eServers
ZENworks	A family of directory-enabled system management products from Novell.

ABOUT THE AUTHORS

Dr. Mansoor Al-Aali has published over eighty research articles, book chapters and books in many areas of computing in international journals and with leading publishing establishments. He has over twenty years experience in systems development and consultancy where he analyzed, designed and managed the development of numerous major computer systems. Dr. Mansoor worked as a consultant for a number of local and international organizations to help in selecting their IT professionals and in advising on training certifications. Dr. Mansoor is now the Dean of Student Affairs at Ahlia University, Bahrain.

Ms. Samia Yousif holds MSc and BSc degrees from the University of Bahrain as well as CCNA, CCNP and CCDA from Bahrain Training Institute. Ms. Samia has developed extensive knowledge and skills in various technical fields in Computer Science and IT. She has published conference publications and books and received e-Government Excellence Award (e-Education Award). She has been selected for reviewing books by a publishing company. She has delivered several IT workshops and attended many seminars. Samia has eight years teaching experience at undergraduate level in CS and IT. Furthermore, she has worked on the development of numerous systems and professional website applications using the most up-to-date web technologies. Ms. Samia is now a Lecturer of Multimedia Science at Ahlia University, Kingdom of Bahrain and she is planning to undertake a PhD program.